Lake Effect

Lake Effect

RICH COHEN

ALFRED A. KNOPF

NEW YORK

2002

Grateful acknowledgment is made to the following for permission to
reprint previously published material:
BMG Music Publishing: Excerpt from "Let's Live for Today" by
Giulio Rapetti and Norman David Shapiro, copyright © 1997 by
BMG Ricordi S.P.A.—Rome (SIAE). All rights for the United States on
behalf of BMG Ricordi S.P.A.—Rome (SIAE) administered by
BMG Songs, Inc. (ASCAP). Reprinted by permission.
Bug Music: Excerpt from "Built for Comfort" by Willie Dixon,
copyright © 1960, 1992 by Hoochie Coochie Music (BMI) / Administered
by Bug. All rights reserved. Reprinted by permission.

Library of Congress Cataloging-in-Publication Data
Cohen, Rich.
Lake effect / Rich Cohen.—1st ed.
p.   cm.
ISBN 0-375-41132-1
1. Teenage boys. 2. Fathers and sons.
3. Male friendship. 4. Chicago (Ill.). I. Title.
PS3603.O48 L35 2002
813'.54—dc21   2001038605

Manufactured in the United States of America
First Edition

For my friends on the North Shore

AUTHOR'S NOTE

While *Lake Effect* is, in essence, a true story, in telling it I have changed most names and many details and, in a few exceptional instances, the course of events. Otherwise, I might have given the impression, wrongly, that I was after a kind of objective truth; in reality, these stories are subjectively told through my eyes and through my memory. Nor have I tried to tell the full and complete story of any of the people in my life. After all, almost everyone I know, even my very oldest friends, remain, in important ways, a mystery to me. I was instead after the spirit of a certain season and the thrill of a certain kind of friendship and what happens to such friendships when the afternoon runs into the evening.

Lake Effect

Part One

In summer we slept on the beach. We would park our cars on a side street and hike through the trees to the ravine and then down to a secret little shore that only we knew about. We would get a fire going and drink red wine and look at the lights winding along the north coast and, to the south, at the haze above Chicago. Out on the lake, we could see the red hazards of ships, and sometimes a speedboat splashed its tiny wake onto the rocky sand. Jamie told stories about the lake, which he said was over a thousand feet deep, and about the ships that had gone down beyond the horizon, voices vanishing in the cold water. When the wine was gone, we sat talking about girls and fights, or what we would do next week or next month. Who could see beyond next month?

There were a lot of us on the beach, the usual crew.

Tom Pistone, who wished he had been a teenager in the fifties, drove a '61 Pontiac GTO, walked with a swagger, and dated girls in polka dots. Ronnie Flowers, who tagged after us like a mascot, was simpleminded and easy to fool and knew just one way to deal with people—as the butt of a joke. Tyler White, a genius or a fool, spent hours watching construction sites.

Of all those friends, the one I remember best is Jamie Drew. Looking back, I see that Jamie was the true hero of my youth, the most vivid presence, not only of my childhood but also for kids up and down the North Shore. Words he said, gestures he crafted, swept our school like a craze, imitated, in the end, even by the teachers. He was quick and dashing and honestly the smartest person I have ever known, and yet he seemed to hold his own talents in mean regard. My mother called him a lost soul. For a long time, I saw him as a tricked-out racer rusting in the garage—that part of each of us that did not survive the rough transition into adulthood.

When the fire burned down, we buried the embers and settled on the sand, which stayed warm for hours. In the morning, the sun appeared across the lake and, one by one, we climbed the hill to our cars and drove home to top off our sleep in our warm beds. Jamie and I often dozed late on the sand and then swam up the shore to the public beach, where our friends, showered and shaved, were waiting.

This was in the middle of the 1980s. It did not seem like it at the time, but that decade, as odorless and colorless as a noxious gas, came to inhabit every part of our lives. On the radio, we listened to "Scarecrow" by John Cougar Mellencamp, each of us worrying, in his own way, about the plight of the American farmer. In the fall, we wore jean jackets and chewed tobacco—Skoal long cut. On the weekends, we disappeared on end runs to Wisconsin, where the drinking age was eighteen, returning with a case of Pabst Blue Ribbon or Point beer. Jamie's favorite beer was Mickey's Big Mouth, which he drank in noisy, head-clearing slugs. We would hide the beer in my back-yard, bringing it inside only when my parents left town. A six pack might make a half dozen trips from the yard to the fridge. When a can was finally opened, it fizzled and foamed with the sweet skunk taste of summer. On television, we watched David Letterman, who was then still funny, and Ronald Reagan, whose smiling face beamed down on us. We knew that Reagan also was from Illinois, but his state and our state seemed far apart in time and place. My father called him the man with the very old face and the very young miracle hair. In school, Jamie and I studied all this in Popular Culture, a class where we also learned stereotypes from entertainment history. Our favorites were the Old Nat stereotype, which resulted in courtly black gentlemen dancing on white movie screens, and the Fu Manchu stereotype, featuring Oriental tyrants hellbent on world domination. Sometimes, as we sat on the beach, a Japanese kid would walk by and Jamie would say, "Think he suffers from the Fu Manchu stereotype?"

Most days ended with a dozen friends back at my house, sitting around the kitchen. I was at first flattered by the appeal I had for my friends, until I realized it had nothing to do with me; my friends were coming to see my father. My father was different from the other fathers in town: men in gray suits, newspaper under an arm, waiting for the train to the city. My father wore dirty brown pants and T-shirts crossed by lines and a watch on each wrist. "A man with one watch thinks he knows the time," he would say. "A man with two watches can never be sure." He had a job that kept him on the road. If not working, he was at home weeks at a stretch, wandering the house in reading glasses and boxer shorts. He often wore a suede cowboy hat, which, he said, identified him as a High Plains drifter. When a friend of mine, accustomed to the routines of his own father, crinkled his nose and asked, "Mr. Cohen, what is it you do?" my father wiped a plate and said, "Son, I am what you call a house husband."

A few years before I met Jamie, his father had been killed in one of those pointless high-speed tragedies that stain our national highways. Now and then, when Jamie mentioned the accident, he would curse under his breath. For this reason, he developed a special attachment to *my* father, who, rather than advise or instruct, simply treated him like a man. More than anything, Jamie was a boy raised by women, by his sister and his mother and his grandmother. I once warned him that a boy raised by girls had a greater chance of going fag. It was a stupid thing to say and a joke, but it turned into a big fight. I guess I was oblivious to the great fearful need in Jamie, the need for authority, someone to guide him. It was a need I would come to recognize in so many of my friends, kids who came of age during the divorce boom, in a nation seemingly without adults, a nation dedicated to the proposition that nothing counts except celebrity; it was this need that would later send us flitting from mentor to mentor, party to party, scene to scene, never resting, never settling, never satisfied with ourselves. For a time, it was a need Jamie and I filled in each other. One night, when he was lying in the twin bed across from mine, after we had each gone through the list of the girls in school we wanted to sleep with, Jamie said, "I wish I could be more like your father: you know, a High Plains drifter."

I laughed. "Jamie, it's just a fucking hat. He's from Brooklyn."

Jamie said, "Yeah, but still, I wish I could be that way."

In the autumn of 1972, my family moved to Glencoe from Libertyville, a farming town in northern Illinois. We were the only Jewish family in Libertyville. When I asked my father if he had met with much anti-Semitism, he smiled and said, "Are you kidding? When we moved in, the neighbors shook my hand and said, 'Thank God, we were afraid they would sell to Catholics.' They hadn't even worked their way down to us yet." Before Libertyville, my parents, newlyweds out of Brooklyn, had lived in New Jersey and Long Island, moving as my father was transferred. As a result, we came to have that special closeness of families on the go. I was four when we left Libertyville. My only memories of that town are of a sunny main drag of car dealerships and Dairy Queens and of the Des Plaines River, which wound by our house. Once, to convince my brother it was safe to walk on the frozen river (in school, my brother had been warned of black ice), my father jumped up and down, breaking through the ice into the swift current. The other things I remember are from stories later told to me: myself, in a red snowsuit, floating face down in a sewer of runoff, where my sister had dropped me; being crammed up the shirt of Tracy Hawkins, a neighborhood girl who wanted to pretend she was birthing me; driving with my mother to see a house she liked in Glencoe, which, in my mind, plays like a fancy movie dissolve into the next scene.

Glencoe is thirty miles up the lake from Chicago. It is a perfect town for a certain kind of dreamy kid, with just enough history to get your arms around. It was founded in the early 1800s by a blacksmith named Taylor, who walked out of the city, dark buildings and foundry flames at his back, into the great silence of the north, forests of oak and elm, Lake Michigan appearing and disappearing beyond the trees. He waded streams and passed through Indian settlements teeming in the open fields—settlements remembered today only in the names of country clubs that, until recently, did not allow blacks or Jews. In a flat place between the lake and the swamps to the west, he cleared trees and built a house and a dock and invited his friends and family to join him. He called the town Taylorsport, a name later changed to Glencoe. For a time, it was an industrial center, where lumber and coal were stacked on barges and towed down the lake. By the 1880s, it was a bustling country hamlet of unlit dirt roads. At night, the sky above the lake was a canvas of stars. In 1892, the town was destroyed in a cattle stampede, a thousand head of raging beef bound for the slaughter yards of Chicago. Ten years later Glencoe had reemerged as a prosperous village of feed stores, blacksmiths, and schoolhouses. When the railroad was built, with a station in Glencoe, the town was yoked to the city. The president of the railroad built a mansion in town.

When my family moved to Glencoe, it still had the character of a village, a life removed from urban turmoil. In the summer, we went without shoes under a canopy of trees along trim midwestern streets lined with Victorian and Tudor and ranch houses. In the woods, there was a bridge built by Frank Lloyd Wright, the only bridge he ever designed, that cut over a steep green gorge. In town, we would wander into stores where the owners knew our names and the names of our parents. Some considered Jamie a bad kid and followed him through the aisles.

There was Ray's Sport Shop, a dark cave cooled by an industrial-sized fan, naked metal blades cutting the air. Ray, in sweat-stained short sleeves, greasy brown hair, and a wispy mustache, thrived on fear, on the terror he spread to the kids in town. If he saw you in a brand of shoes not sold at Ray's Sport Shop, he waited for your mother to walk into a store, grabbed the meat of your arm, and said, "I run a family business. Maybe I don't sell the best stuff, but I sell it only to you kids. If you don't buy my stock, my family starves. Get it?" A few years later, when Ray sold out to a Korean immigrant, the kids of town, free at last, went on a magnificent mall spending spree. There was U-Name-It, a store that surfed the T-shirt craze, pressing decals of Arthur Fonzarelli or designs that said HOCKEY MOM or I'M THE GREATEST AND KNOW IT. I had two shirts that identified me as A WILD AND CRAZY GUY. There was Harry's Delicatessen, where my father often ducked out back to smoke a cigar with the owner. The walls of Harry's were lined with pictures of regulars, including Jamie's mom, who was a secretary in a doctor's office in the city. Once, when I wanted to complain that my father was not on the wall, Jamie said, "Why not let my mother enjoy this glory alone?" There was Sloppy Ed's, a hamburger stand where we stopped every day on the way home from the beach. Sloppy Ed himself was a sort of guru, sweating over the grill and cursing the kids who came in just to play the video games—Frogger and Donkey Kong.

We lived on a plateau north of town, in an upscale area known as the Bluffs, down a winding street buckled by tree roots, in a drafty brick house built in the 1920s. It was a rambling collection of back stairways and secret rooms. For years, my parents did not have enough money to furnish the rooms and every word echoed in the emptiness. As a result, the house felt like a piece of scratch paper, something you scribble on and throw away. When I was older I played floor hockey in the basement and, using markers and spray paint, filled the walls with the faces of spectators and scoreboards and dreaded hecklers. I covered the floor with the boulevards and buildings of a major city. Starting with a piece of Astroturf, I built a cemetery, with overturned garbage pails standing as tombstones, each recalling the life of another dead eight-year-old—my age at the time.

Soon after we moved in, my mother led me through the street, from house to house. I had to knock on each door and say, "Hello, I am new in the neighborhood. Are there any kids here I can be friends with?" It was torture. After several misses, we came to a blue wood house down the street. Before I knocked, the door opened. There was a short roly-poly kid: big mouth, giant teeth, bright eyes, dopey grin, fluttery hands. His voice was high, persistent, excited. It said, "My name is Ronnie. I'll be your friend. Best friend. I love friends, love 'em. Don't got many. See that car over there? That's a Valiant. It got top marks on the test track in Chamonix. My house is old. Let me get my stuff. My butt hurts. Can I sleep over?"

Ronnie was the first friend I ever made. Every day, before school or on weekends or after school, he would come over to our house, knock on the door, not leave. If the door was open, he did not bother to knock and you would come across him in the halls, smiling, waiting to say, "See that car out there?" Or "Want to hear the funny thing about this jar?"

Sometimes, my mom would find him in the kitchen and say, "Ronnie, Richard is not home."

Ronnie would say, "That's OK. I'll play with Herbie."

One afternoon, when Ronnie was standing in the downstairs foyer, my father—Herbie—spotted him from upstairs. Stepping into the shadows, my father cupped his hands and, in a voice that boomed through the empty halls, said, "Ronnie, this is the Lord thy God."

Ronnie looked up and said, "Yes, God. I hear you. Where are you, God?"

"Ronnie, I will not reveal myself to you yet. You are not ready. You must first go home and ask your mother to read to you from the Bible. Go home, Ronnie."

In town a few weeks later, my mother ran into Ronnie's mother, who said, "We've got Ronnie in counseling. He thinks he spoke to God."

I walked to school each day with Ronnie and my brother, Steven, who is five years older than me. In those days, my brother worshiped my father and imitated everything he did. When my father threw out an old briefcase, my brother fished it out of the trash, patched it, and cleaned it with a miracle product ordered from television. So there I was, between a roly-poly Ronnie and a twelve-year-old with a briefcase full of book reports. In this manner, I went grade to grade—from the Explorers to the study of mold. One morning, a gym teacher named Bowman, a crew-cut ex-Marine with whiskey breath and dark glasses—during lunch period, he sent me to buy him smokes in town—told my class, "In high school, you are in for a rude awakening. You'll be walking down the hall and a senior will hit ya and ya'll hit the floor and he'll keep on walking."

I remember thinking, At least he won't stay around to kick me.

Then I was at New Trier, a rambling high school backed by fields and running tracks. There were floors and floors of classrooms and a swimming pool and a theater and gymnasiums and a fenced-in smoking area for bad kids and an auto shop also for bad kids and a power plant with smokestacks rising in a winter sky. It was the typical American high school, with kids swimming by in tight schools—green schools of football players, black schools of theater geeks, tie-dyed schools of Deadheads. When a school of football players passed through a school of theater geeks, there was a flurry in the water, a commotion of charley horses and arm slugs. New Trier is where

John Hughes set his movies about teenage angst: *Sixteen Candles, The Breakfast Club, Ferris Bueller's Day Off.* We were often told that it is the best public school in America, a citadel of success, where every kid goes on to college and the good life. We were taught the names of the many celebrities who were graduates: Ann-Margret and Rock Hudson, Bruce Dern and Charlton Heston. We were warned of the pressure of such an environment—not everyone can be a Rock Hudson—and guidance counselors reminded us that our school district was the center of the teen suicide belt. I had a teacher named Tony Mancusi who introduced himself to us, saying, "Kids, my name is Tony Mancusi, but call me the Cooz. The door of the Cooz is always open; whether you want to discuss a grade or a teen pregnancy, do it with the Cooz."

There were more than four thousand kids in school. In those first months, people who had been stars in junior high school might rise quickly through the ranks and just as quickly flame out, sputter, and die away. Other kids simply vanished, falling to the bottom of the food chain— you might ask after them at the Dr. Who Club. For much of high school I just let myself be carried by the current, lost and drifting, searching for interesting faces. One of the best friends I made was Tom Pistone, whom I met junior year in gym class, first period swimming, toeing the line in our damp school-issued Speedos, taking orders from a mustachioed, comically vain teacher everyone called Magnum P.E. On the weekends, Tom built cars from scratch, and he loved the fifties. At my house, my father looked Tom up and down and said, "You remind me of a kid I grew up with: Bucko. Bucko was the coolest kid I knew."

Tom grinned and asked, "What is Bucko doing now?"

My father thought a moment, then said, "Last time I saw Bucko, he had a gun and was guarding a junkyard and listening to calls on his police radio."

One afternoon, as I was moping through another bleak winter day, Tom looked at me with his earnest drive-in stare and said, "You ever meet Jamie Drew?"

"Who?"

"Drew-licious. C'mon, you'll get a kick out of the kid. He's absolutely crazy."

Actually, I had already heard of Jamie. He had moved to Glencoe from one of those working class towns west of the city, a ragged collection of liquor stores and laser-straight streets tucked behind the slaughter yards. His name was Jamie Drew, but in the seventh grade the girls started calling him Drew-licious. He was preceded by a legend. He was the kid you see late at night, walking the streets of a town, shadowed by police cars. When he was eleven, he had been arrested for breaking into cigarette machines.

Tom led me to a homeroom on the far side of the school. We looked in the door. A teacher was sitting at a desk reading a newspaper. Some kids were in front doing homework. The rest of the class was in back, gathered around someone at a desk. This was Jamie. As he talked, the kids in front stopped doing their homework and the teacher put down his newspaper. Jamie had recently read *Tortilla Flat* by Steinbeck and so spoke in the mock-heroic manner of the characters, an errant knight of King Arthur's court. Rubbing his belly, he laughed and said, "Surely our friend will not begrudge us a single beer, for he is our friend and must certainly know that without beer we will not have the strength to fight evil."

Tom waved and said, "Drew-licious."

Jamie waited until the teacher was looking the other way, then ducked out of class. He put his arm around Tom and said, "Hey, buddy." We were just sixteen, but already you could see how handsome Jamie was going to be. He had high cheekbones and a long nose and his eyes were dark and restless; his hair fell to his shoulders in curls, and his skin was smooth and coppery. There was a tireless energy about him, an inquisitiveness that made him fill in the border of each scene. Before listening to a story, he had to know dozens of irrelevant details. "Where did it happen? How did you get there? Did you hitch? What did she look like? Does she have a sister? Cousins? A brother? How much can that dude bench? Who's from Waukegan?" If he was excited, he slapped his knee. If he was very excited, he slapped your knee.

Jamie looked at me and said, "So what's up?"

Tom introduced us. Jamie narrowed his eyes and said, "Yeah, I know you. You're from the Bluffs." He did not say how he knew me. It did not matter. We were already friends. Tom, having made the connection, now drifted into the back of the scene. And so began my adventure with Drew-licious, and with it a new stage in my life.

I began spending most of my days with Jamie. We met each morning outside the school rotunda, where hippie kids played hackey-sack. I told him stories about my house, things my father said, how my mother reacted, or else about the letters I received from my brother, who was then in his cool phase, which blew through our lives as brief and refreshing as a tropical wind. That fall my brother had entered New York University, where he hung around the Cedar Tavern, let his hair grow into a dizzying 'fro, rarely shaved, drank Jim Beam, and read Jack Kerouac. He sent pictures. Before first bell, Jamie would examine each shot, studying the facades of Greenwich Village. "How can you beat that," he would say. "Fucking New York!"

We often met during school, in front of the office of the student paper, the *New Trier News*, where I was a beat reporter. The room was filled with long tables where the newspaper was laid out, and the walls were lined with cubbyholes where, each Monday, I received my assignment. The assignments were made by Doc Tangier, the faculty sponsor, a strange old queen with a long face, pale skin, eyebrows shaped like boomerangs, and a goatee years before the return of the goatee. I was also in his English class, a seminar where, every morning, another classic (*The Secret Sharer, All the King's Men*) was picked apart to reveal its secret homoerotic theme. One day Doc Tangier asked us, "Do you still use the word 'tool' when referring to an erect penis?"

A football player said, "No, we use the word 'lilyrod.' "

Doc Tangier, who knew and approved of my sister years before, took an instant disliking to me. He selected me to cover the Ham Radio Club. When Jamie read my article about the uses of ham radio, including communication in the event of a nuclear apocalypse, he said, "So if Armageddon comes, the only remains of the human race will be these guys talking to each other?" On one occasion, I was suspended from the paper, punished for my story about a New Trier football game, during which the Glenbrook North marching band had been driven from the field by a hail of pennies. I defended the rowdy crowd on grounds that the marching band was wearing painfully funny hats. Doc Tangier fixed me in a cold stare and said, "Mr. Cohen, you are not the smartest person in the world, but then again you don't pretend to be."

Jamie would sit in the newspaper office, looking over my shoulder, saying, "No, man, compare the ham radio kids to visionaries trying to raise God by computer."

Doc Tangier did not mind having Jamie around, and I often caught the Doctor looking at him. "Your friend is not unlike one of those pained heroes of Greek literature," he told me. "One of those wondrous young boys who reach their potential only after a terrible fall from grace."

Sometimes, Doc Tangier gave us permission to walk the halls, to roam with the freedom of my press pass. The classrooms flashed by, rows of boys in oxford shirts, girls in stone-washed jeans, teachers who stepped into the hall and said, "Back to class, Drew-licious." Jamie talked mostly about sex, some new revelation, how he got a girl's shirt off. He was still smarting from his breakup with a senior, a girl with a car, a beautiful girl in jeans and lip gloss, who one day, as inexplicably as a change in the weather, went punk, turning up for school in a green Mohawk and black lipstick. Kids who envied Jamie the day before shook their heads and said, "Poor bastard." For my part, I envied Jamie even his pain. So what? He loved and lost. I had never even taken love out for a soda. Once, as we were crossing the parking lot behind school, a girl walking the other way smiled at Jamie and Jamie smiled back, and she flipped up her skirt and I could see her legs and her underwear and it was really something to see. Jamie grabbed my arm and said, "Don't worry, friend, you'll get in the game."

During free periods, I met Jamie in a basement common room, where you could buy doughnuts and soda. The walls were covered with murals painted by students during the Bicentennial—snare drums, flags, and flutes. At each table, kids chewed tobacco and spit into soda cans. When a kid, reaching for his Coke, grabbed the wrong can, a howling filled the room. There were also narcs on the prowl. A paraprofessional would sit at your table, rub his eyes, and say, "Fuck, man, I am harshed! Do you know where I can score some weed?"

For the most part, the talk was of sports, with betting pools on every game, or of girls. A kid named Randy Klein told a crowd how, anxious to lose his virginity, he had visited a prostitute in Chicago. Before Randy had sex, the prostitute asked if he wanted to do anything else. He said he wanted to "try that sixty-nine thing." As a result, Randy had to rush home, feeling ill and still very much a virgin.

Jamie and I sat at a table in back, where we were joined by Tom Pistone or Ronnie. Letting his gaze drift across the room, Jamie would give a name to each type of kid. He did this in the manner of Adam in the Garden of Eden naming God's animals. This gave us a sense of strength, of mastery over the school; by naming, we took possession of what we had named. There were, of course, the Football Players and the Cheerleaders and the Honor Students, but, according to Jamie, there were also the Big Dumb Guys, the Little Dumb Guys, the Girls of the Big Dumb Guys, and the Speed Walkers, who, with their minds fixed on college, did everything extremely fast. "Dig that," said Jamie. "Never a wasted move."

Then there were our friends, who also fell into categories. I had played hockey since I was young, so there were the kids I met on the ice in Squirt or Pee Wee. These friends liked to watch the Chicago Blackhawks on cable television or the video of *Slap Shot,* the Paul Newman movie about minor league hockey. They looked at Jamie with suspicion, a slickster never tested on the boards or on the field—Jamie had no talent for sports. As I came out of the locker room after a game, hair wet from the shower, carrying my bag and my sticks, Jamie was waiting, his hands thrust deep in his pockets. He would shrug and say, "Let's get away from these clowns."

Through Pistone, we were also friends with the gear-heads, who smoked cigarettes which they tossed away with a flick, lifted weights, and haunted the low-slung garages of West Wilmette. Leaning over engines, they would raise a hand and say, "Now really wind her out." These kids were strangely war-haunted. They wore fatigues to school and dog tags and talked about fighting Charley. A kid named Glenn Christian, who later joined the Marines, told me he was the reincarnation of an American who died in Khe Sanh. I laughed. The next day, he came to school with the death certificate of a soldier killed on August 15, 1968. "The day before I was born," said Christian darkly.

"Why the day before?" I asked. "Why not the same day?"

"Don't be an ass," said Christian. "Reincarnation takes at least a day."

In movies about high school, there is always the

shadow of something ahead, the Vietnam War or the threat of adulthood, but in our lives there was nothing but clear water into the distance.

And there were the girls from Glencoe, a pack roaming in the streets of town. Jannie Ruffan, who had blond hair, a freckled nose, and a laugh that climbed your spine like fingers; Carrie Sharp, a cute redhead who appeared in a touring company of the musical *Once Upon a Mattress;* Haley Seewall, whose mother thought I was a hoodlum and who, for no apparent reason, insisted on calling me "Deacon." These were our girls, who, like a free space in bingo, we did not have to work for or luck into or worry about. As a result, we came to see them as off limits to the general population—off limits even to each other. These were good girls, whose chastity, unbeknownst to them, we had vowed to protect.

Around this time, one of the football players, a squat mean-faced kid named Motu, met a man in a bar downtown, a man named Rizzo, who invited the football player to bring five boys and five girls to his house for a game, "Rizzo's Game." A week later, five football players took five girls down to Rizzo's, where they undressed, sprayed each other with whipped cream, rolled around on the floor, ate bananas, showered, and went home. The story of Rizzo's house spread through school. At the end of the month, the same five football players asked Haley Seewall, one of our girls, to play Rizzo's Game. Jamie begged Haley not to play. "If you go," he said, "I will never talk to you again."

Haley went to Rizzo's, and the school was soon filled with stories of the dirty things she had done. When Haley tried to talk to Jamie, he waved her away. A few days later, he told me there was too much talk in general. "What is all this chatter?" he asked. "I sit in class and listen and listen, and then a teacher asks me a question that she damn well knows the answer to and I gotta spit it back? I say no."

"You say what?"

"I say up to this point yes, beyond this point no."

The next morning, when I met Jamie outside the rotunda, he would not talk to me. I was offended until I realized he would not talk to anyone. For one week in March, Jamie did not say a word to his family, or friends, or teachers in school. When called on in class, the kid at the next desk would say, "To cleanse his system of the modern world, Drew-licious will not speak for five days." Even the teachers came to respect Jamie. When at last he opened his mouth, his voice was clear as a bell. "So this is how I sound," he said with wonder.

Haley ran over and hugged Jamie. He turned away. That was fifteen years ago and he has still not said a word to her.

A few months after I first met Jamie, he invited me to his house. As usual, we hitchhiked from school, getting off at Green Bay Road and cutting through town. In college, far from the Midwest, I would draw maps of Glencoe,

each avenue and throughway. Looking at those maps, I
would imagine Jamie and me walking that winter afternoon along the lake bluffs, the sailboats pulled up onto
the sand. It was very cold. Following the advice of parents
everywhere, I was dressed in layers. Jamie wore only a
T-shirt and a cloth jacket. He said it was important to look
cool, even if it meant freezing to death—an ethic he
brought with him from beyond the slaughter yards. Jamie
was a lower-middle-class kid living in an upper-middle-
class town. This made him seem authentic and interesting. In him, I found a vitality and an excitement that my
family's relative affluence had sealed me from. In me, he
found the stability missing from his own life. He also
found an audience. Shivering in the wind, he clapped his
hands and said, "In my mind, I'm on a beach in the
Azores."

Jamie lived within sight of town in a trim, two-story
wood house in a neighborhood of brick behemoths. It was
white with green shutters, and there was a backyard with
flowers and shade trees and a garage, where, a few nights a
week, Jamie and Pistone pieced together an old Mustang
convertible. Jamie lived on the porch, an extension built
under the trees—an arrangement that allowed him
incredible freedom. Late at night, if he was restless, Jamie
would climb out his window and into the street, where
Pistone was waiting in his GTO with the lights switched
off. Dropping the car into gear, Tom would coast off to a
college party or a double date or to Big Twist and the

Mellow Fellows, a band who played at Biddy Mulligan's, a bar on the North Side of Chicago. As the sun came up, Jamie was back in bed, drifting off to the whistle of the commuter train.

In Jamie's room, there was a desk covered with pictures. In one, Jamie was dressed as a priest. He had his pants pulled down and a beautiful Chinese girl was spanking him with a rubber chicken. Jamie looked at the picture and said, "Someday I'll tell you the story." Another picture showed a handsome man with powerful shoulders in jeans and a leather jacket and a cowboy hat pulled low. The sky behind him was filled with mountains. I assumed this was Jamie's father but did not ask. I have always found it difficult to bring up any subject that might make anyone, especially a friend, unhappy. As a result, I come to know people only over the course of time, and only by seeing their personalities played out in a dozen tiny incidents.

Jamie took the photo out of my hand and set it back down on his desk. He crossed the room and opened his closet. The shelves were like something from a downtown boutique, with shirts arranged by color, earth-tone to pastel, and button-downs in perfect rows. He bought these clothes in secondhand stores—silk shirts decorated with stripes or teardrops or painted designs. As we spoke, he stripped off his T-shirt, folded it neatly, and, for a moment, stood bare-chested, scanning the shelves. He was at ease with his body, which was as well formed as the hull of a ship. I became conscious of my own torso, which, in comparison, seemed to me a failed prototype. He smiled as he carefully took down a black shirt patterned with red dice. It draped smoothly across his shoulders. "My Dean Martin look," he said. "Brings me luck."

"Is there a reason you need luck?"

"Well, for one thing you're about to meet my grandma."

Since his mother worked downtown and his sister was never around, Jamie was often alone with his grandmother, Violet, a willful old lady with a puckered face and sharp blue eyes. Years before, Violet had moved to Illinois from a small town in Nebraska. To her, Jamie was a boy with too much spirit. To Jamie, Violet was big government, whose laws are best read as suggestions. "Yes, I love her, but she drives me nuts," he would say. "She has to have her hand in everything."

We sat at the kitchen table, where Violet set out pound cake and orange soda. In school, we studied Mikhail Gorbachev and the Russians and the nuclear stalemate we knew would go on forever. Jamie was one of the few kids who took none of it seriously. As I chewed, he leaned over and said, "Want to see a real Cold War?"

Jamie sipped his soda and set down the glass. Violet moved the glass an inch closer to the center of the table. Jamie took another sip, and again Violet moved his glass. Jamie winked at me and said, "Violet, I am now going to take a drink and return my glass to the spot which you have chosen. To prove you love me, do not move my glass."

"Why would I move your glass?"

Jamie took a swallow and set down his glass. I looked at Violet. I could see the battle she was fighting within herself. When Jamie looked the other way, she moved the glass. "Aha," said Jamie. "I have seen you. Why can't you just leave well enough alone?"

In a whispery voice that was like music, Violet said, "I don't know."

It was clear that Jamie was locked in a comic struggle with his grandma, a struggle that reached its apex years later, when Violet mistakenly believed she had won the Illinois State Lottery. Over the course of a summer day, she and Jamie, closed up in the house, traveled the spectrum of emotions from devotion to complete distrust. When I showed up, Jamie told me, "Though I am not ready to kill Violet for the money, I am prepared to convince her that it should be transferred to my name for tax purposes."

A few hours before dinner, Violet hid the ticket, saying, "No one will ever find it."

"You are an old lady," said Jamie. "What if you die? Then no one will ever get that ticket. Did you think of that?"

Violet looked at Jamie and said, "I don't know."

.   .   .

Whenever I think back on Jamie and the life of his house, it is Violet's voice I hear, a lyrical plea that pursued Jamie through the halls. "Jamie? Where are you, Jamie? Have you forgotten your grandma? Jamie." It was this voice that chased Jamie into the streets, in and out of a dozen stores, and through the spring slush to my house, where he began spending more and more time. You entered my house through the kitchen, where you might find my father in beetle boots and reading glasses, eating ribs or stone crabs or ice cream. When I brought Jamie home for the first time, the door opened on a strange scene: my mother in a neck brace, which she wore when suffering from one of a dozen mysterious ailments. Without a word of hello, she said, "Have you seen your father?"

"No," I told her. "I just got in."

She walked out, and a moment later my father came in, opened the fridge, and asked, "Is your mother looking for me?"

Before I could answer, he left with a chicken leg. Then my mother was back without the neck brace. She went to the freezer, took out a bottle of vodka, poured three fingers, tossed it off, and walked out. My father came in, smiling, sharing a joke with himself. He looked at Jamie and said, "Who is the new kid?"

"This is my friend Jamie."

"Richie has always had real trouble keeping friends," said my father. "I don't know why. But for God sakes, son, be careful."

Then my father went out and my mom came back in, wearing the neck brace. "Is your father looking for me?"

Without waiting for an answer, she left the room.

Jamie said, "Is it like this every time?"

I said, "It gets worse."

Ducking out of the kitchen, we made our way through the house, from the dining room to the living room, which had finally been furnished with chairs and tables that went out of style the moment they were delivered; to the library, filled with law books and plays by Eugene O'Neill; to the family room, that staple of suburban life, which had once been my bedroom but was now filled with couches and video games and an Apple II computer on which my father did not balance accounts, my mother did not store recipes, and I did not write term papers; through the red room which, before college, had been my brother's, and the pink room which, before college, had been my sister's—rooms as empty and forlorn as once-vibrant immigrant neighborhoods abandoned for better streets in the suburbs; through Dolmi's room, the live-in housekeeper from Ecuador, who had dressed up her wall with a tremendous crucifix, an exotic presence in our otherwise secular home; at last we made our way to my room in the attic, that wild terrain north of the second floor.

In my house, the attic had always been the frontier, the country where a man went in search of freedom. There was a couch, a television, a stereo, two single beds, and a window that opened onto a flat roof. In the summer, we would climb onto the roof, smoke cigarettes, and blow smoke over the gables and dormers of the Bluffs, the dark lawns and rusting basketball hoops, blue light flashing in windows where parents flipped from *The Tonight Show* to *M*A*S*H*. "This is the real Glencoe," Jamie would say. "And when I am old, this is how I want to live."

Since the situation at Jamie's house was less than ideal, he was soon sleeping at our house three or four times a week, in the single bed a few feet from my own. Sometimes, in the middle of the night, he would wake me up to talk about a dream or a girl he could not stop thinking of. Or else he would speak of his childhood, the years before his father died, long long days around the house, like they were some kind of Eden. He spoke too of the state trooper arriving with the tragic news, and of his sudden consciousness of the sadness of the world, which he called his own personal fall from grace, as tormented and anguished as the fall of Adam. "You see, every man inherits the Fall but every man relives it too," he told me. "Every man passes through all stages of man, as the embryo of a baby—and this is something doctors can actually see—passes again through all the stages of evolution."

One night, when Jamie excused himself from the dinner table, my father, home from a business trip and too tired to care much about anything, said, "It seems like that Drew-licious kid is here a lot."

My mother said, "Jamie lives here."

My mom began to treat Jamie like a member of the family, asking after his schoolwork, making sure he was home early on weeknights. We worked side by side in the attic, dashing off papers, clowning, and chewing tobacco. Now and then, after he had been around for several days, Jamie would simply disappear, meaning he had hooked up with a girl or stumbled upon some adventure. He might be gone for two or three days, but he always came back, in a clean shirt, smiling, telling stories. On those occasions, I was jealous of Jamie, of the places he went without me. My own existence, compared to his, seemed half lived. Often I greeted him with silence or cursed him for leaving me behind. "Oh, c'mon," he would say. "Your time will come."

"When?"

"When you're ready."

But I could not stay angry at Jamie and was soon laughing at his jokes or asking him to repeat some off-kilter observation. "When you watch an old movie and you see a dog, did you ever stop and think that every one of those dogs is dead?"

Finally, the last day of junior year, as kids tore up their textbooks and lit fireworks in the hallways at school, Jamie said, "Tell your mom you're sleeping at my house. I'm taking you out and getting you drunk for the first time. That way, even when you are an old man, you will still think of me."

After school, I showered and put on a blue shirt with yellow stripes. Looking in the mirror, I asked myself, "Will Jamie like this shirt?" I said good-bye to my mom and went outside. At seven o'clock, I heard Ronnie say good-bye to his mom, start his car, and then he was at my house.

A few years before, tired of taking schoolyard abuse, Ronnie had put himself on a strict weight-lifting program. Bit by bit, he had turned into a stocky, slow-moving monstrosity. He wore T-shirts that hugged his biceps and spoke mostly of cars, of turning radius and zero-to-sixty. When he got his license, he told us, he would soon be driving his mom's vintage Porsche Spyder. His father, a serious Christian, instead gave him a car that had once belonged to his church group, a roomy blue Plymouth with yellow vinyl seats. Rather than complain, Ronnie put a happy face on this development and spoke of the size of his engine block. To prove his point, he jammed the accelerator and sent the car flying. Driving with Ronnie was harrowing. In his car, people actually fought to not sit up front. Once, riding shotgun with Ronnie, I struggled to fasten my seat belt and did get it fastened the moment before we hit a tree. Walking around the smoking ruin, he said, "It is not nearly as bad as I thought." Jamie had asked Ronnie to drive only so we did not have to worry about drinking. In those days, Ronnie would do anything for Jamie. Like everyone else, he wanted to remake himself in the image of Drew-licious.

"What about this shirt?" Ronnie asked me. "Will Jamie like it?"

We drove through town to Jamie's house. When Ronnie hit the horn, I said, "Sounds like my grandma's horn."

Ronnie said, "Want to take a look at the engine block?"

After a while, he turned off the car and we went in. Violet was standing in the doorway. She asked Ronnie to sit down and then walked around him like he was a tree. "I cannot believe it," she said. "How did you get so big?"

Ronnie did a sort of aw shucks thing, then said, "The gym."

Violet put her hand to her mouth and said, "You mean you did this to yourself on purpose?"

As I walked upstairs, I could hear Ronnie ask for something to eat and Violet say, "You've had enough."

I found Jamie in the bathroom, sitting before a steamy mirror, brushing his hair. His reflection looked back through a porthole cleared in the mist. He was wet from the shower and his body glistened; he wore white boxer shorts covered with dollar signs. "What do you think," he asked. "Too boastful?"

I sat on the edge of the bathtub and watched as he ran a razor under his chin. He had no hair on his legs and his chest was smooth. He opened a bottle of cologne, smelled it, made a sour face, closed the top, and said, "I prefer my own smell."

He pulled on a pair of cloth pants and a shirt that was

the orange of the sky at sunset. He took a last look in the mirror and ran downstairs, where Violet was wide-eyed, head in hand, listening to Ronnie. "I do twenty reps of flies," he was saying. "Then squats, then bench. And I gotta find a spotter, 'cause the weight I lift is heavy duty. So you know what I do?"

"No," said Violet.

"I carbo-load."

Jamie grabbed Ronnie and a moment later we were in the Pontiac, heading south on Green Bay Road. We picked up Tom Pistone, whom we found in the garage behind his house, working on an engine with his father, who was young and blond-haired and handsome and wore a one-piece jumpsuit. Compared to my own parents, he was a strange comic-book creature.

Wiping grease from his hands, Mr. Pistone cleared his throat and said, "Boys, I know you're taking Tommy out for a big night, and why not? I also know that boys your age get hopped and blow your cool and, if a girl is present, maybe go off too soon, sometimes in your pants, to your shame and to the girl's endless frustration. What I am saying, boys, is: For Chrissakes, have patience!"

He reached into his jumpsuit and pulled out a hand-rolled cigarette.

"So to help you, I invite you to share this joint, a hit or two of which will keep you calm and loaded for bear."

"What is it?" I asked.

"It's the finest creeper weed, boy. Take a drag, and

twenty minutes from now it sneaks up on you and *pow*! Takes you where you want to be."

Tom said, "Dad, I asked you to stop pushing that shit on my friends."

Tom's father shrugged, lit up, and ducked under the hood, vanishing in a cloud of smoke.

And we were back on the road, heading east, flying by cookie-cutter houses and overgrown parks, by kids walking home from Little League, cleats clattering on the pavement, or else entire teams, in jerseys marked with the names of sponsors—Marcus Opticians, Olsky Jewelers, Bressler's 33 Flavors—celebrating a victory with two scoops. We rolled down the windows and a breeze blew off the lake, and it was sweet and filled with the summer ahead. Ronnie turned on the radio. We argued over the station. Tom wanted to listen to the oldies, Buddy Holly, the Everly Brothers. His favorite song was "Let's Live for Today," by The Grass Roots. Sometimes I caught him singing the words under his breath: "Sha na na na na, live for today. And don't worry 'bout tomorrow, hey, hey!" I liked WLUP, the Loop, which played music that made you feel good about being born in Middle America— Springsteen, Petty, Cougar. Jamie wanted WXRT, which was New Wave and Punk. Ronnie liked the Beach Boys, but Ronnie did not have a vote.

After a while, Jamie put his head out the window and looked at the sky. The stars were out. "Late enough," he said. "Let's go to McDonald's."

McDonald's was in the town just south of Glencoe; it had opened a few years before, amid much protest. The more staid elements of the community feared the fast food chain would upset the bucolic mood of the north suburbs. There were mass mailings, protests, meetings. In the end, the restaurant won approval in a referendum. To the kids it was VE Day, cheers and low-fives, uninvited kisses in high school hallways. In the first flush of victory, the owners of the restaurant agreed to build in the manner of the local architecture, with no golden arches and no big sign, the building as modest as a Swiss chalet. We called it Mickey's or McDick's or Mickey D's—a frequent stop on our aimless nocturnal rambles.

On weekend nights, kids from the shore turned up at the restaurant. They stood in the parking lot or sat on car hoods or crowded in front of the cash registers. There was endless conversation—what happened at school or what happened out front, a fight that had changed the social hierarchy. Mostly, there was talk of parties. You went to McDick's when you wanted to find out whose parents were out of town. Standing in the parking lot, you heard about a party, drove over, drank until the cops broke it up, and then headed back to McDick's.

"Let me do the scoping," Jamie said as we walked in. "I'm gonna move around and be careful and not hit on any party that is too soon to be overrun or that has been sniffed out by the McPig."

The McPig was Chico Ronga, an off-duty cop that McDonald's hired to manage the weekend crowds. Chico carried a blackjack and a walkie-talkie, wore polyester pants and a mustard yellow windbreaker, and greased his hair back. He had a skinny waist and a tremendous gut, which he carried like a pot of gold, saying, "Out of my way, you little fuckers, or I'll pulverize ya!" Chico was a working-class guy from the west suburbs. He hated the rich kids on the shore; he hated their manner, their clothes, their foreign cars; he hated their parents; mostly he hated that they called him the McPig. Each night he would eavesdrop. If he heard of a party, he called it in to the Winnetka police.

Chico liked Pistone because they raced their hot rods on the same track. As Jamie walked through the crowd, Chico threw his arm around Tom and said, "Tommy, boy, ain't seen you and your old man out at the course."

"Don't worry," said Tom. "When we come, we'll come heavy."

Chico laughed. "I'll pulverize ya!"

Jamie walked over.

"What about it?" asked Tom. "Any parties?"

Jamie looked at Chico and said, "Let's get something to eat."

Chico said, "The kid ain't talking in front of the McPig."

We took a booth. Jamie said there was a party in West Wilmette at a kid named Jake's house. "Good kid," said

Jamie. "And he has some kind of home-fermented shit we can try."

Ronnie said, "I can't drink. It inhibits muscle mass."

As we were talking, Terry Montback came over with a tray of McNuggets. Montback was a forty-year-old guidance counselor from school; it was his job to talk to kids, listen, gather information. Sliding into our booth, he said, "How's it hanging, Drew-licious?"

"What's going on, Mr. Montback?"

"Just thought I could take a chow with you guys."

Like so many adults, Montback admired Jamie, the kid he could never be. He asked about our final exams and about our families, then moved on to his only real subject—the difference between his generation and our generation. "Just look at almost anyone under twenty," he said. "What do they care about? In my time, we marched on Washington and protested Vietnam. Kids today care about nothing."

Jamie frowned and said, "It is not that young people now care less than young people then. We're just not as stupid."

"How do you mean?"

"In your time, you believed in your government, that it was good, that it would serve you," said Jamie. "So when you became adults and saw that the world is corrupt, you took it as a personal insult. You thought, 'My God! The world is corrupt! I must cure the world!' So now, when you look back and see people like me who have no interest in being shocked or in curing the world, which, as you yourself learned, cannot be cured, you think we are lazy. But we're not lazy. We're smart. We know that the world is corrupt, that it always has been, and that it always will be."

"So you'll do nothing?"

"Well, I won't become hysterical," said Jamie. "I won't convince myself that my personal discoveries are like the discoveries of Columbus. I won't insult a generation of strangers by calling them lazy."

Montback got up and walked away.

A few minutes later, we were back in the car, driving into the flat, featureless towns west of the lake. We sped through open fields, the soft wind whispering in the cattails. As we crossed the highway, looking south we could see Chicago on the horizon like a thunderhead. The west faces of the tallest buildings glowed in the sunset. When we reached Wilmette, Jamie guided Ronnie, saying, "Left. Past the gas station. Cut through the cemetery. Think of the dead lying in the ground. Watch for the speed trap."

So the cops would not be tipped off by a street filled with cars, we parked a few blocks from the party, walked through backyards, and made our way to a wood house, as simple and insubstantial as a drawing in crayon. We knocked. For a time, we stood looking at each other in the porch light. A girl opened the door and said, "Drewlicious!" She led us down a hall to a room filled with music and conversation, boys holding bottles of beer by the neck, girls angling glasses to cut down on foam. It was like stepping into a speakeasy. I felt the excitement of being away from my parents, with new friends, far from the pettiness and humiliations of my past. Jamie said, "I'm gonna find Jake."

Tom wandered off, and for a time, I was left alone with Ronnie. He pretended to talk (brake pads), and I pretended to listen, but both of us were really watching Jamie. The party had broken up into smaller parties, groups of people in the kitchen and in the living room, gearheads around a car in the garage—the engine racing, falling silent, racing. Jamie danced from crowd to crowd, welcome in every group, too restless for any single conversation. We were still years away from cocaine, and yet, as he ran through the rooms, he looked like a speed freak, determined to let nothing pass him by. He wanted it all and he wanted it now.

He found Jake in the garage and brought him over to me, saying, "This is Jake. This is Jake's house. In the basement of Jake's house is a bottle of home-brewed whiskey fermented by Jake's brother, who is off in the city with the big kids. Jake has invited us to drink this poison together with him."

Ronnie said, "Is it safe?"

"Nothing is safe," said Jamie. "That's why we do it."

Ronnie said, "My body is my temple."

Jake said, "It won't kill you."

Jake wore overalls with nothing underneath and greasy hair pushed back and no shoes. His front tooth was chipped. He struck me as a sort of suburban Huck Finn, fiddling under the hoods of abandoned cars, sleeping on the beach. To him, everything was comical, and he laughed at the slightest suggestion of a joke. That night, he made me feel like the funniest kid alive, guffawing at my observations on the suburbs, house parties, the nature of man. Jamie said, "OK, funny boy, are you ready to drink this hooch?"

The basement was standard issue: damp, spooky, pachinko machine, board games (Risk, Pit, Sorry), washer-dryer. Reaching behind the dryer, Jake retrieved an unlabeled bottle filled with murky yellow liquid. He unscrewed the cap, breathed in the fumes, and grimaced. He took a deep breath, as if he were about to dive into cold water, and drank. He wiped his mouth on his forearm and handed the bottle to Jamie, who took a slug and passed the bottle to Tom, who said, "No fucking way," and passed the bottle to me. The whiskey had a rotten smell that I recognized from car trips through Gary, Indiana.

Jamie said, "Hey, Richie, whatever you want to do, that's cool."

I closed my eyes and took a swallow. It was sharp and clear and I could feel it burn going down. I imagined it glowing in my stomach. When I passed the bottle to Jake, he said, "One's enough." Jamie took the bottle, drank, handed it to me. I drank and handed it to Jamie. He drank. I took the bottle back and downed a big slug.

Jamie said, "Go easy."

He balanced the bottle on his leg. I grabbed it away and started to drink. Jamie grabbed me, saying, "Enough." He pulled the bottle out of my hand and smiled and said, "Jeez, you want to go blind?"

In my memory, the next several hours are as ragged and gap-filled as a home movie shot on super eight: I am in a kitchen, talking to a girl, who holds my hand and says, "Go on, please go on"; I am on a weedy lawn, looking at the stars, tears running down my face, saying, "None of it means anything"; I am in a parking lot, shoving a kid, throwing a punch, and getting knocked down; I am on a public beach, kids gathered around a bonfire, which sends smoke into the sky; I am wading into water so cold I cannot feel my feet; I am rolling in the sand. And all the while I am aware of Jamie, never more than a few feet away, watching me. Though I am stupid and helpless, he keeps me close and protects me from the bad things that can happen to a young kid drunk on moonshine.

Jamie carried me up the steps to the parking lot and gently laid me in the backseat of Ronnie's car. In those days, Ronnie was mostly interested in driving fast. He often used the term *red-line*. "I red-lined this baby at one-twenty-five." At the same time, he was petrified of getting a ticket or of any other run-in with the cops, who he feared would abuse him as he had been abused on the schoolyard. So, believing a patrol car hid on every side street, Ronnie would gun his car up to a hundred miles an hour and then brake down to thirty-five in time for the intersection. That night, hanging out the window, my head rattled around like a Ping-Pong ball. When we reached Jamie's house, I crawled out of the car and puked in the bushes. Jamie took me behind the garage and stood me against a tree and took off my clothes. When I opened my eyes, I saw Jamie ten feet away, aiming a hose at me. The water came in a cold blast and I hugged myself and coughed and shouted, "I am not an animal!"

Jamie dried me with towels. "My mom and Violet are asleep," he said. "So be quiet as you walk through the kitchen." When he opened the door, I ran naked through the house, threw open the door to his room, and dove into his bed. Even before I landed, I was fast asleep.

When I opened my eyes, it was eleven in the morning, the sun was shining, the windows were open, and a warm breeze carried the smell of cut grass. I was a seventeen-year-old kid the morning after his first drunk, and I felt fantastic.

I asked Jamie for my clothes.

"I put them in a bag," he said, "and threw them very far away."

"Even my shoes?"

"Especially your shoes."

Jamie gave me a shirt and a pair of shorts and we walked to town. The doors of the stores were open and the merchants stood in the sun. We ducked into Ray's Sport Shop, which had been failing since Ray sold out. The new owner, Lee Ho, a Korean in his forties, was extremely happy to see us. As we walked the aisles, Lee pushed his glasses up his nose and, in a singsong voice, said, "Best nylon, two-ply," or "Cross training, training two sport," or "Racket wins while you enjoy tennis."

I picked out a shirt, a bathing suit, and shoes. I asked Lee to send the bill to my parents, a service performed by every store in Glencoe, making life, for the kids of town, the very best dream of communism.

As Lee put my shorts in a bag, he said, "OK, do you want to wear your old shoes or your new ones?"

I said, "I have no old shoes."

Lee tossed his head back, burst out laughing, and through his laughter shouted, "No shoes? You really need new shoes!"

Jamie and I started laughing, and we were still laughing as we stumbled out onto the warm sidewalks of town. And all at once, I realized this was a windy June morning, the first day of vacation, the entire summer before me, a new country waiting to be explored.

Jamie said, "Let's go to the beach."

So we turned onto Hazel Avenue and started east, the lake waiting at the end of the road. I thanked Jamie for taking care of me the night before and told him I was embarrassed about how I acted. "It's not your fault," he said. "It's these towns. There's nothing to do so you go and get blind drunk and then suffer the remorse. No. There is only one way for us. As soon as I get the Mustang running,

we're heading down to the city. That's the place. That is
where it will all happen. In the city."

Of course, we could get a lift into the city from Ronnie,
but that would mean having Ronnie along with us, and
in that case we would be better off in the suburbs where
the inanity of Ronnie at least had its proper context. It
was not just me who believed that, in a showdown with
Ronnie, Chicago would be in some way diminished. So we
waited, kicked around, followed my father through the
backyard, gleaning his routine for some pearl of wisdom—
"Remember, boys, if you don't know where you're going,
any road will get you there"—as each night Jamie and
Tom, whispering and passing tools and opening beers and
stepping into the street to watch the moon set over the
low roofs of town, worked on the car, bringing it around,
piece by piece, gear by gear, like a great holy ark that
would carry us to another world. "Look at her," Tom
would say. "I can see my face in the fender, my god-
damned beautiful face."

One afternoon, as I was standing in my driveway,
throwing a tennis ball at the garage, practicing the many
trick pitches that my father had taught me (screwball,
knuckler), I heard what sounded like a gunshot followed
by laughter and a beautiful hum. When I turned around,
Jamie and Tom, side by side in the Mustang, were daz-
zling under the overhanging trees. Across the street, an

old man was watering his yard. In the spray, I could see a thousand tiny rainbows. When the Mustang pulled up, I could hear, blasting from the speakers, the opening words of "Let's Live for Today." *When I think of all the trouble people seem to find, and how they're in a hurry to complicate their minds . . .*

Tom turned it up and shouted, "I even got the fucking tape deck to work."

Inside, the car was like a cockpit, the low-slung driver's seat surrounded by dials and warning lights. Behind the stick shift, Jamie had installed a phone, an old piece of junk found in his garage. It connected to nothing. At stoplights, if he pulled alongside a car full of girls, he would hold the phone to his ear and take up a conversation left off at the last stoplight, a never-ending argument with his agent. "No more openings," he would shout. "I'm only human."

Jamie looked at me, alone in my driveway, and said, "Let's go."

"Where to?"

"The city."

I ran inside, changed my shirt, pulled on a pair of clean pants, ran some water though my hair, looked in the mirror—not bad—told my mother I was going to Jamie's house . . .

"When will you be back, honey?"

"I'm sleeping over."

. . . ran outside, climbed into the backseat, and said, "Onward."

Jamie threw the car into drive, scooted past Ronnie's house—I could see him in the window, watching with his sad, sleepy eyes—and then we rolled through town. We went by Ray's Sport Shop and Harry's Delicatessen. There was a line outside Sloppy Ed's, the girls in constellations, moving through their galaxies. To the kids of town, Chicago was a place seen two or three times a year from the window of a Town Car or from inside a restaurant; now here we were, lighting out on our own. Under my breath, I said, "Going to the city. Got business in the city."

We followed Green Bay Road to Sunset Ridge, which took us through the lagoons of the Forest Preserve and then onto the Edens Expressway. With the shudder and pace of the passing cars, I at once felt I had slipped the bonds into another world. To this day, I feel the same on an airplane bound for a foreign country. I am on the ground in New York but, surrounded by accents and a mood of excitement, I'm already on the far side of the ocean. I never saw Jamie look in the rearview mirror or check his blind spot or look in the side mirrors, and still he seemed to know just where we were on the highway. He dodged the slower traffic like it was standing still.

We sang along with the radio and talked about the girls in school and the difference between the juniors and the sophomores; then about white women and black women and which is better in bed (Jamie said he definitely wanted to sleep with a woman of every race); and then the best kind of beer, Mickey's or Point; then nuclear war and would it be better to be at the epicenter of the blast or out in the suburbs, where you would stumble around for a few days and then die. Jamie said he hoped to be vaporized and leave behind nothing but his shadow.

About thirty minutes south of Glencoe, the trees along the road gave way to factory yards, billboards, and smokestacks. Jamie turned down the radio and there was only the sound of the wind. I looked at the passing neighborhoods—neon signs, pool halls, apartment houses, clothes strung over yards, fathers over barbecues, smoke mounting into the clear summer sky. I thought of the families sitting to dinner and wondered why I had been born where I was born and why my parents were my parents, and I was soon imagining the life I might have led in one of these town houses, the elevated train rattling past, the city at the end of every street.

Up ahead the sun was going down and the skyline of the city looked like a paper cutout against pink marble. We got off the highway at Ohio Street and rolled by apartment houses and traffic lights to Michigan Avenue, gliding between the tall buildings, coasting along the canyon bottoms. Tom knew the name of each building; he pointed out the Playboy Club, roguish with its peaked cap; the Tribune Tower, a sandcastle at the mouth of the

Chicago River, and the John Hancock Center, saying, "That's the sixteenth biggest building in the world." Tom already had that brand of pride characteristic of Chicago, a pride built on insecurity, a fear that people in the East are laughing at you. For this reason, anyone from Chicago can give you a tour organized around the phrase *Biggest in the world.*

"See that fountain, Buckingham Fountain? Biggest in the world. Even bigger than the one they got over in England. See there, those stockyards? Biggest in the world. And it's not even close. See that? It's the Sears Tower, biggest building in the world."

Looking up to where the sky was still blue, I felt like a reef fish peering at the surface of the water.

"Where are we going?" I asked.

"The South Side," said Jamie. "The Checkerboard Lounge."

Everyone I knew was afraid of the South Side. The name itself was a curse, a slander; it struck fear in the heart of every kid from the northern suburbs. It had once been the home of our grandfathers, a haven for immigrants from Poland, Russia, and Greece. On weekend nights, the air had filled with fumes from their grills— souvlaki, bratwurst, sausage—and the streets had soaked up the warm midwestern rain. But drib by drab the sons of those immigrants had moved to the manicured pastures of Rogers Park or Bucktown, or even farther north to Winnetka, Evanston, Glencoe. And so the South Side had become a great American slum, a ramble of burned-out buildings and tenements, the hunting grounds of black and Puerto Rican street gangs, the Latin Kings, the El Rukins. It was where TV reporters filed their most troubling reports, where cops went for kickbacks. It was where you headed if you had nothing to lose, if things could get no worse, if you were out of ideas and did not mind being beaten or robbed or kidnapped or killed. It is where, on our first night in the city, Jamie had decided to take us.

"Why?" asked Tom. "In the name of God, why?"

Jamie parked on the shoulder of Michigan Avenue, put an arm around Tom, and explained how, on the South Side, we could mingle and carouse with the true aristocrats of the city, and also we would not be carded.

"That's your reason?" asked Tom.

"That, and because we are going to hear the blues, and there is no place to hear the blues but on the South Side, and because there is really nothing closer to my heart tonight than the blues."

Before Tom could think of an answer, Jamie started the car and made the wide turn onto Lake Shore Drive. It was the moment when the chain catches hold on the roller coaster. Tom whispered, "Oh, fuck," and the buildings flew past, following the curve of the shore. We ghosted by the Shedd Aquarium and Soldier Field and exited in one of those featureless neighborhoods just beyond the Loop, rocky little beaches and grimy apartment towers, and then we were into the real South Side, gliding down end-less avenues of storefronts, boarded brick buildings, and check-cashing joints with one light burning.

We turned onto 43rd Street and pulled up before a dilapidated house—the Checkerboard Lounge. If only I make it inside, I thought. There was a steel chain strung across the front door. A big man in a black coat looked me up and down and said, "Five bucks." I handed over the money and stepped into a rank-smelling room just big enough for a stage, warped under weak lights, a few dozen chairs, and some long narrow linoleum-topped tables. The room was crowded with hipsters from another era, black men of the 1940s celebrating the end of the Second World War, in velvet pants and candy-colored jackets and wide-brimmed hats and, below the hats, smiles filled with gold teeth. The women wore jumpsuits and tottering-high heels. Walking to the bar, in groups of two or three, their asses swung like metronomes. They returned with glasses of syrupy red wine called Ripple and ice-chilled shots of Chivas Regal. There were a lot of beauty products in the air. If the storm fronts of perfume and cigarette smoke had met, it would surely have rained inside the club. Now and then, the men burst into laughter.

"What are they laughing at?" I asked.

"Us," said Tom, who was making eye contact with a bus of a man with long Jheri Curls. On his right hand, he wore one of those rings which says a name (Terrence) and stretches across three knuckles and is just the best thing for fighting.

"We're not such a big noise that they need to talk about us," said Jamie. "These men talk about rivers."

Jamie ordered three glasses of Ripple and three shots of Chivas. I swallowed a mouthful of Ripple. When it reached my knees, I was happy. I smiled at a woman and she smiled back. Tom rolled his eyes. Jamie said, "No, it's OK. He's just feeling it and there is nothing less real in feeling it than in not feeling it."

And then Jamie was feeling it too, and so was Tom, and a few of the fellows got on stage and picked up instruments and started to play. The singer sat on a stool, a big man in overalls. His voice was scratchy and his belly shook as he shouted, "Some folk built like this, some folk built like that, but the way I'm built, don't ya call me fat, 'cause I'm built for comfort, baby, I ain't built for speed."

When I went to the bathroom, I saw Jamie in a corner talking to a guy in a green suit. Jamie followed me into the toilet and said, "C'mon, we're leaving."

"I just ordered another Chivas."

"Finish your Chivas and we're gone. There's a guitar player on the West Side, a place called Rosa's, supposed to be the best guitar player in the city. His name is Melvin Taylor."

And then we were back on the road, rushing past row houses frozen in the moonlight. Jamie fooled with the radio, then shut it off. He spoke about the blues. He said the blues had come from the South, from farms and plantations where field hands strummed acoustic guitars. He said the blues had followed the Mississippi River north, picking up the rhythm of the cities as it went. He said, "That is why, in the best songs, like 'Bring It on Home,' by Sonny Boy Williamson, you can hear the freight train and the highway." He said the blues eventually reached Chicago, where Howlin' Wolf and Johnny Shines worked as night watchmen in factories and added to the music the sound of the slaughter yards and the assembly lines. He said major innovations came in downtown clubs where it was too noisy to hear acoustic instruments, so the musicians plugged into speakers. He spoke specifically of Muddy Waters, who ran a Coke bottle up and down his guitar strings, and of Little Walter, who electrified his harmonica, giving it a lonely late-night sound. He told us the names of his favorite singers: Robert Nighthawk, Johnny Littlejohn, Lafayette Thomas, Hound Dog Taylor, Little Milton. When he stopped talking, we were in front of Rosa's, a neon sign flickering in the window.

Rosa's was dank, a bar running down one side, a stage in back. Drinks were being served by a quarrelsome old lady with a shock of white hair. The place was empty, a few aficionados lazing in their cigarette smoke. Onstage Melvin Taylor was playing guitar with his band. He wore a beautiful shirt and dark blue pants, a hat pushed back on his head. On the guitar strings, his hands blurred like propellers. With each guitar burst, his eyes widened. His fine-boned face opened and closed. He sang about drinking and chasing girls, being chased by girls, and satisfying many women at once. His music was like nothing I had ever heard—guitar solos cool and precise and running out like surf.

We finished our beers and ordered more and then the music had us on our feet. Jamie threw an arm around me, the lights of the city spinning behind him like a trick in an old movie. His breath was hot and beery. He said, "Check out the bass player, the ass on him. He's got big pants not as a statement of fashion, you understand, but because those are the only pants that can handle that tremendous ass—an ass handed down from generation to generation—and it is awesome and majestic, like a state flower, by which I mean a symbol of something else, a whole republic of guys out playing the blues in bars." Then he said, "What would Chicago be like without black people? A wasteland. And to me that big ass is a symbol of this other city thirty miles from home, but we never see it, and that is something I will drink to."

In that moment I understood, for the first time, that Jamie and I had come together on a quest. I suppose we were searching for grittier terrain, a world more real to us than the suburbs, a place where the paint and paper had stripped away. Jamie was my guide on this search, for his life seemed more genuine than my own, more genuine and more interesting.

Melvin Taylor finished his set, went behind the bar,

and poured himself a drink. Jamie walked outside and came back with the car. We drove to the Edens Expressway and headed north. The morning fog was rolling in. The buildings of the city were lost in the fog, and I could see the tops of the towers suspended. Jamie's eyes glazed over, but when I nudged him he said, "I'm just fine." And soon we were back in Glencoe, on empty roads, streetlights shining in the fog.

That summer we had no jobs and no desire to find jobs and did nothing but try to impress each other. It was our work. Hours, days, weeks went by with nothing but a perfect sense of stillness. There would always be time—time to wander, time to waste. Most days, we slept late, walked to town, met at the counter of Sloppy Ed's, filled up on hamburgers, and then went to the lake.

There was a pier called Ming Lee's, a broken-down dock with boards missing and, at the end, a steel structure that must have once been a house. I was never sure why it was called Ming Lee's, but some kids spoke of a crazy old Chinaman who had been seen emerging from the water stone dry. We would sit at the end of the dock smoking or drinking. Kids climbed the ruined house and dove off into the lake.

One afternoon, Darren Faulkner, one of nine brothers, the red-haired bullies of our town, made the climb. It seemed that there was a Faulkner for every grade and a brother was assigned to you along with a homeroom. *Mr. Evans is your advisor, Kyle will be beating you up.* There was Kyle and Kit and Tim and Buddy, who formed a club called "The Committee to Derail the Train" and who actually went to work on the problem. We always half-hoped something terrible would happen to the Faulkners, and that afternoon Darren jumped into the water and did not come back up. He hit a pole hidden beneath the surface. It broke his neck. The accident cursed Ming Lee's and made it into one of the mystical places along the shore.

A few hundred yards down the beach, we had a favorite spot, a spit of land that ran out into the clear water. Stretching a towel on the sand, Jamie would watch girls go by and talk about Ronnie Flowers. Jamie had a talent for studying people, picking apart their behavior. It was as if, by studying other people, he hoped to find clues to his own life. He might discuss the tribulations of Ronnie, or his chances of future success, or his prospects of love. Jamie's favorite subject was the destruction of the old Flowers house, which had burned down years before—a fire spotted by my brother, who noticed, on a hot summer day, smoke coming from the Flowerses' incinerator chimney. My father rushed over to the house, rang the bell, banged on the doors, and then, trying to get inside but also because it must have been fun, tossed a heavy piece of lawn furniture through a picture window.

Within a few hours, while the Flowerses, at the Ice Capades, watched a Smurf turn a double axel, their house was consumed. In its place, the family built a behemoth, a New Age shoe box of a house set amid gardens of bad sculpture.

"I have a theory, controversial, so bear with me," said Jamie. "I think Ronnie's father, Bob, Bob Flowers—I think Bob set that fire. Think about it. The Flowerses were in their forties, shackled to a very tired routine. Life was behind them. Then their house burns down. Heirlooms, antiques, photographs—all of it, the whole past with its cargo of failure and disappointment—gone. They are free! So what do they do? The dumb bastards, they build another house, another trap, and they think they can finesse it by building a house that is absolutely modern, up to the minute and all that. So now they are stuck with a new life that was new in 1976.

"It must have been tough for that kid," Jamie went on. "It must have been like growing up on the set of *Kojak*. Never allowed to touch anything. I've probably been in that house five times, and never once have I seen Bob Flowers. I mean, I've heard his voice: 'Ronnie, tell your friends it's time to go home!' When Bob drew up the plans he must have engineered it acoustically so that, while lying in bed, he could yell at Ronnie no matter where he was in the house."

In the afternoons, we piled into Jamie's car and just

drove around. Sometimes we went to one of the underground record stores we discovered in that gray area where the city shades into the suburbs: Round Records or Vintage Vinyl or Wax Tracks, dingy head shops with hookahs and water pipes and know-it-all clerks. There was always a good record on the stereo, but you were too proud to ask for its name. Jamie went straight to the racks of funk and blues, too cool for his own time. Standing over the records, hair falling below his eyes, he would say, "Reverend Davis! Man, that's it! The true gen!"

I searched for imports by the Kinks or the Rolling Stones or the Who. In this, I was pretty typical. I also liked Bruce Springsteen and was forever on the lookout for bootlegs of his legendary shows at the Bottom Line in New York or at the Roxy in San Francisco. On those records, you could hear the voices of people in the audience, and it was not hard to imagine the smoky clubs. I liked it when Springsteen drifted in and out of a song, telling the boardwalk stories of his boyhood on the Jersey shore. I believed he was singing about the life we were living—the summer life.

We went back to my house, sat around the attic, and listened to our records. In the summer, the floor creaked and the wind blew. Sometimes, as Jamie talked about the meaning of some obscure verse, I would record him on video tape. (I had borrowed the camera from C. C. Durst, a tough fireplug of a kid, and returned it years later when it broke.) Onscreen, Jamie looked like a second-tier movie star, the vehicle of a late night mystery. I featured him in a movie called *The Humiliator,* in which he played a white-collar bully. In the course of the action, I am paid to humiliate him and do so with nothing but a cup of luke-warm water and impeccable timing. I used Jamie in *Cross Now,* based on *Apocalypse Now,* in which Jamie, once a promising young crossing guard, has gone wild in the forest, giving people bad directions and crossing them into the very teeth of traffic. In the last scene, I termi-nate Jamie's command. And then *The Embarrasser,* a sequel to *The Humiliator,* in which Jamie and I humiliate the Embarrasser. I am especially proud of the training sequence.

When Ronnie went on a vacation, we filmed *Ronnie Doesn't Live Here Anymore,* in which several people remi-nisce about Ronnie, including a postal worker, who says, "I hardly knew him. Sometimes I saw him playing basket-ball. Do I miss him? It would be unfair to say, but I do wish he were here." When Ronnie returned from his vacation, we filmed *I'm Sorry,* in which Ronnie apologizes over fifty times: to his parents, to his friends, to his teach-ers ("It was my fault I couldn't learn; I'm sorry") to his neighbors, to himself, to his cousin ("You should've been born first, anyone can see that; I'm sorry"), to a toll booth attendant, to a man on the street, to a guy on a road crew ("It's not the jackhammer, it's me, I'm a light sleeper; I'm sorry"). In each movie, I tried to capture a true piece of my world and to show the laymen, if the laymen were interested, what it is like to grow up down the street from a kid like Ronnie.

When it was too hot for the beach, we went to the city to see the Cubs. This was more me than Jamie; he was not really a fan. The notion of being an observer, of sitting and rooting for someone else—well, that was just not Jamie. To him, spectator sports were a kind of mass hysteria during which regular people turn themselves into a crowd. "There is nothing worse than a crowd," he said. "Everything bad that happens happens in a crowd." I told him there is a lot to learn from a crowd. It always seemed to me that you got closest to the real Chicago in the stands of its stadiums. After a Bears game in January, a playoff that the Bears lost, which therefore marked the onset of true winter, I was in a crowd of fans crossing Lake Shore Drive in gloomy end-of-the-season silence. The mood lifted only when, out of nowhere, a gruff cop with a tremendous mustache said, "Get your heads up. Tomorrow's another fucking day."

One afternoon at the end of the summer, I took Jamie to see the Cubs play the St. Louis Cardinals. We met in town, caught a bus to Evanston, and stood on the platform waiting for the train. Jamie handed me a silver flask, which he had tucked into his pants. It was dinged up with impressions left by fingers and marked with the initials J. D. "It was my father's," said Jamie. "It was his before the tragically unfair accident that ended his promising young life." Whenever Jamie spoke of his father, it was in a kind of heroic tone that often struck me as a put-on.

There was whiskey in the flask. When the train came, we sat in the last car getting drunk. At each stop, more fans crowded aboard with pennants and spongy WE'RE NUMBER ONE fingers. Heading south, the train threaded its way through a private world of red brick and fire escapes, curving in and out of apartment houses with quick glimpses of kitchens and living rooms. Jamie opened a window—you could do that on the El—and stuck his head out. Behind him, the images of the city spun past: street signs, billboards, aerials. He closed his eyes. I asked a question. He ignored me. I asked again. He ignored me. I grabbed his shoulder and pulled him inside. An instant later, a brick wall dashed by the window, not two inches away.

Jamie turned pale. It took him several seconds to find his voice. He said, "I would have been cut in two. Right now, my head would be bouncing around somebody's yard. You saved my life." He was quiet for the rest of the trip, looking out the window. When the doors opened, we followed the crowd.

Wrigley Field is at the intersection of Addison and Sheffield avenues on the North Side of Chicago. It is a tight configuration of brick and wood, an heirloom of the last century. It was first home to the Chicago Whales, of the old Federal League. I told Jamie about the great athletes who, over the years, had played in the stadium. Mike Kelly was a hard-drinking Irishman from the South Side, the first catcher to think of communicating with his pitcher in a code of often comical hand signals. Cap Anson, a true racist, described a minority hire in his autobiography as "A little darkey that I met in Philadelphia, a singer and a dancer of no mean ability, and a little coon whose skill in handling the baton would have put to blush many a bandmaster of national reputation. I togged him out in a suit of navy blue with brass buttons, at my own expense, and engaged him as a mascot." Grover Cleveland Alexander, a once-great pitcher, came back from the trenches of the First World War shell-shocked and broken. A heavy drinker, Alexander fell into seizures on the mound. On such occasions, the infielders shielded him from view and made certain he did not choke on his own tongue. In the bio pic, Alexander was played by Ronald Reagan.

My favorite old-timer was Hack Wilson, a squat alcoholic power hitter who still holds many offensive records. After a storied career, Hack Wilson became a drifter, wandering from job to job until his death in 1948. His body went unclaimed for three days. Years before, in 1929, when the Cubs lost the World Series, he had told a train terminal of reporters, "Let me alone now, fellows, I haven't anything to say except that I am heartbroken and that we did get some awful breaks."

Jamie and I bought bleacher tickets. The sun beat

down. There were shouts from the concessionaires. In the distance, the empty train rumbled off to the city. We stepped into the shadowy depths of the stadium, a post-card view—grass, dirt, players—at the mouth of each tunnel. Jamie laughed. I suppose he was happy to be alive.

The bleachers are home to the most belligerent fans in Chicago, a mob seated directly above the action. In the course of a game, the hecklers shout and curse. It's a signal achievement to so incense an enemy outfielder that he climbs the ivy—scrambling up the vines that pad the outfield wall to reach the heckler. I was at a game in which Omar Moreno, of the Pittsburgh Pirates, started up the trellis only to be pummeled and covered in beer. One minute he was on his way up; the next minute he was flat on his back. After a game in which the home team was heckled, the Cubs manager, Lee Elia, blew up in a press conference, calling the bleachers "a playground for the cocksuckers." There was even a theatrical production set entirely in the bleachers called *Bleacher Bums,* a play co-written by the actor Joe Mantegna in which, in the course of nine innings, a man falls in love, a kid learns the meaning of life, a bully gets his comeuppance, and the Cubs lose.

Jamie and I found a spot on a bench in left field. The fans in the right-field bleachers were shouting, "Left field sucks!" I could see the broad back of Gary Matthews, the Cubs left fielder whom everyone called "The Sarge," a pot-bellied, pigeon-toed veteran. He was warming up, playing catch with the center fielder, releasing the ball in an easy motion that sent it across the field on a tight line. I watched dozens of games that summer, some on television, some in person; in the course of the season, the Cubs lived a lifetime. I saw blown leads, comebacks, seesaw battles. What I did not read in the *Chicago Tribune* I learned from Harry Caray, who announced the games on TV and radio for WGN.

Harry Caray had waxy white hair and a pink face with a high plastic shine. His heavy black glasses were a trademark, and he slurred in a way that made you think, The old boy has had one too many. His most famous exclamation, "Holy cow!" was used on home runs and double-plays but also on strange and wonderful sightings around the ballpark. Spotting the right sort of woman in the right sort of bikini, he would interrupt himself to shout, "Holy cow!" Or, on another occasion: "Check out the kid in the sombrero! Holy cow!" At times, he seemed to ignore the game altogether and instead talked about a favorite bar or restaurant or a sausage that had set his stomach ablaze. Between anecdotes, he might make brief mention of a spectacular development: "So anyway, this joint, it has a great jalapeño burger—*there's a triple play*—but, Cub fans, this thing *will* repeat on you. Holy cow!"

In the mid-eighties, when the Cubs seemed sure to win their first World Series since 1908 (they blew it), it was Harry Caray who created my sense of the team. He spoke of their all-animal infield. "It's a zoo out there," he would say. "Leon 'the Bull' Durham at first base, Ryne Sandberg, 'the Ryno,' at second base, Larry Bowa 'Constrictor' over at shortstop, and Ron Cey, 'the Penguin,' at third." He said this was not only the most competent infield in the game but also the best-looking. "Sandberg, classical good looks. Bowa: scrappy, sinewy, sexy. Ron Cey: just look at that guy! Bull Durham: what woman would not want to make love to Bull Durham?"

Jamie ordered two beers and struck up a conversation with the girls in the seats next to us. These girls were from one of the towns out near Santa's Village, a stark nowhere by the airport. They wore tight shirts, denim skirts, and white boots—outfits that triggered certain socioeconomic half-truths that I could not put into words. Here is what Jamie was saying: "On the way up here, I almost died. My head, the very head you see sitting atop my shoulders, this one talking to you, it was almost sheared clean off. For all I know, it *was* sheared clean off and this is just a crazy postlude for my brain, which is too dumb to know it is sitting in the bushes in some backyard."

"What are you saying?"

"I might be dead."

"You think you are dead?"

"Can you prove to me otherwise?"

I was irritated. Jamie was letting his attention be drawn from the game. He was mixing up sex with the sacred. I took a slug of beer and reached for his hand. I held it tight. I spoke of my father and how he had told me again and again not to be a fan of the Cubs. He hoped I would instead follow the New York Yankees or the Los Angeles Dodgers, teams he had loved as a kid. He worried that, in following the Cubs, who almost never won, I would come to accept failure as the natural condition. The better the Cubs look, he told me, the bigger the heartbreak.

"So you see what this means," I told Jamie. "If the Cubbies win, I will at last emerge from the old man's shadow."

But Jamie had already drifted back to the girls, who were rubbing his neck and head, assuring him that he was still very much alive. He made a joke and they sipped his beer. One of the girls climbed on his lap. Jamie had a hole in the crotch of his jeans. The girl stuck her finger in the hole and Jamie said, "Be careful, you could get shocked." In this manner, the game drifted by, fly balls carried on the wind, clearing the wall, landing on Waveland Avenue, where a passerby would look up and shout, "Ours or theirs?" If the ball had been hit by the Cardinals it would be thrown into the bleachers, from where it was tossed back onto the field.

In the seventh inning, Harry Caray stuck his head out of the press box and sang "Take Me Out to the Ball Game." Though he had performed this ritual at thousands of games, he mangled the words, singing, "Buy some peanuts and popcorn too!" It did not matter. It was still terrific.

By the top of the ninth inning, dark clouds had rolled in and we could see flashes of lightning. The city glowering in the distance looked like something from a painting by El Greco. With two outs, the Cardinals, who were ahead by a run, loaded the bases. The third baseman came to the plate, banged the mud off his cleats, and waved his bat. It got quiet. You could hear the flags snapping on the flagpoles. The pitcher went through his windup, the batter swung, the ball jumped. The Cubs center fielder, Bob Dernier, standing a few feet behind the infield, ran with the swing. At the end of his run he dove, reached out, and caught the ball. He waved to the kids in the bleachers. From that moment, Bob Dernier was my favorite player, this wiry dude with curly blond hair spilling out from under his hat. He was not an icon. No one will remember his name. He was just one of the boys who flashes for a summer and then drifts back to his shit-kicker town to work in an office by the highway, coach Little League, and grow paunchy. "So I could see this, " said Jamie. "That is why I did not die on the train."

In the bottom of the ninth inning, two Cubs reached base. The wind picked up. Trash blew along the ground. A hot-dog wrapper danced out of my fingers and onto the field. It blew through the legs of the outfielder and was kicked away by the shortstop. The lights blinked on in the press box. The left fielder looked at the sky. A raindrop fell. It stained the dirt on the warning track. Spectators headed for the tunnels. The ground crew stood at the edge of the field. Jody Davis, a Cub with big freckled arms, came to the plate, watched two pitches go by, plucked at his jersey. The next pitch was inside. Jody swung. A flashbulb went off and the moment was frozen in the light: this big kid swinging from his heels, the catcher rising out of his crouch, the sky a moment before the cloudburst. The ball landed a few rows behind us in the bleachers. A guy with a huge gut held it aloft. Jamie said this guy would no doubt open a restaurant and call it The Guy Who Caught the Ball's Place. "People will come in and ask, 'Is the guy who caught the ball here?' And the hostess will say, 'Sorry, he only comes in on weekends.' "

The Cubs spilled out of the dugout and stood around home plate waiting for Jody Davis—just a kid living one of those moments that sports can deliver, a tiny epic, like a feat from a storybook. When Jody reached home plate, he vanished into a shower of back slaps, and the sky opened and it started to rain.

Jamie and I followed the crowd through the tunnels and into the rain. People were cheering and high-fiving. I asked Jamie what happened to the girls. He shrugged. To me, situations like that never mean anything unless they lead to other situations. Jamie said that no other situations were necessary—those girls had already been as much fun as they were ever going to be. As he said this, we were following a sea of wet backs across Addison Avenue to the El. Water ran in channels along the curb. Jamie threw his head back. His shirt was soaked and it clung to the folds of his body, each as carefully drawn as the shadings on a blueprint. I shook the water from my hair and slicked it back. I saw my reflection in the glass of the station door. I felt sinister. Jamie said I looked like a gangster. In the distance, I could hear a roll of thunder. A train was waiting. We piled on and tottered off into the storm. The windows were steamy, and through the glass the passing yards were lush and green. We sped by the wall that almost took off Jamie's head. When I pointed it out, he said, "Are you crazy? Nothing can kill me." With each stop, some more people got off, until the train was just us and a few old-timers heading to the suburbs in the rain.

Jamie and I got off the train in Evanston and stood in front of a liquor store until a guy in the parking lot agreed to go in and buy us beer. He came out with a six-pack of Budweiser. I offered him an extra five bucks, but he refused it. Walking down Green Bay Road, we took turns holding the bag. Cars had on their headlights. Jamie stuck out his thumb. A Volvo stopped and we ran to the car, each with our own fantasies about some lonely housewife, but inside were two girls from school, a year younger than us and cute.

We drove through the little towns along the shore. Jamie talked about the summer and the summer parties and told the girls we had a six-pack and wanted to be dropped off at the Glencoe beach. He asked if they wanted to come along.

One of them said, "In the rain?"

When the girls dropped us off, we could see patches of blue sky. The girls said they would try to come by later.

We walked to the gate where on most afternoons a lifeguard checked beach tags, but the rain had closed the beach and the gate was locked. No one was around. We climbed over the fence and followed a steep road down to the water, walking between the thick oak trees, the leaves dripping with rain. Between the trunks I could see the stormy surface of the lake.

We left our shoes on the road and went across the beach. It was damp and firm. The sand was cool between my toes. In the distance, there was a group of those Midwestern kids who think of themselves as surfers, even though they live a thousand miles from a decent wave. These kids were dreamers, listening to the Ventures and Dick Dale, reading surf magazines, driving around in station wagons loaded with surfboards, and hoping for even a modest storm that might generate a chop. Just now, they were in wetsuits, paddling out into the water. We went the other way, past closed-up food concessions and boats that had been pulled up onto the sand. Jamie went out onto Ming Lee, lay on his stomach, and looked into the water. It was very clear. He dropped the beer and it fell to the bottom, sending up a plume of sand. A gull wheeled far above. The lake smelled fresh and clean.

We walked along the beach. Jamie left his pants and shirt on the sand. His body was like carved wood, with broad shoulders and a slender waist. He was tan. I fol-

lowed him out into the water. The rain started, drops
jumping off the surface. I dove under the water and swam
along the sandy bottom. It was quiet and cool. When I
came up, Jamie was far ahead, swimming against the current. A few minutes later, I climbed onto the raft, wooden
planks with a diving board. Jamie was stretched out on the
raft in the rain. It drummed against his body.

The rain let up and I sat on the edge of the raft, my feet
in the water. The sun shone through the clouds and beams
of light went far down into the lake. I could see mossy
rocks on the bottom. On the surface, the water was as
smooth as glass. Fish jumped. Looking north, I could see
the shore and the houses built into the ravine, white
houses with black roofs, and the wet road with traffic
going along it. Far away, I could see the haze over the city.
In that moment, the lake seemed to me a great ocean,
rimmed by cities and towns, Chicago and Milwaukee on
its western shore, the colleges of Michigan on its eastern
shore, the industrial wastes of Gary and Hammond, Indiana, on its southern shore, and, on its northern shore, the
blue-black forests of the Upper Peninsula, with its
sawmills and ragged docks. I thought of the ships sunk
deep in its canyons, skeletons in the galleys.

Jamie sat up and said, "Over there."

Far up the beach, holding a shopping bag, were the two
girls who had dropped us off. Jamie called out to them,
waved, and went off the diving board. I could see his body
knife through the water, sharp and clear, gliding along the

bottom. He came up once, took a breath, and dived back down. The next time he came up holding the beer, which by now was cold. He walked along the shore, hugging himself. He called to the girls. I slid off the raft and swam to the beach.

And those strange overcast afternoons that would come in the middle of the summer, in the very hottest part of the season, as a respite or a remission, with the lake churned up and a cold wind, so much colder for being out of place and unexpected, blowing in from some far-off north country. The kids would wander through town in sweatshirts and long pants and flip-flops, huddling in the diners and the record shops; or stand on the beach in the damp wind, the kind of wind that has always made me certain there is no God or, in another mood, that there is a God; or wade into the surf—yes, in the Midwest, we call it surf—which on those cold days always felt so wonderfully warm. It was those afternoons that made you see the summer as fragile and precious and transient, and compared to them the hot days were a mindless idyll.

One evening, as I was driving home, coming up the rise that climbs into the Bluffs, moving into the thicket of houses, each with its own story and its own parents and its own kids—and at this stage in my life I considered it my job to know every one of those stories—I forgot, for one strange moment, just who I was. I am not suggesting that my mind failed, or that I suffered from some kind of amnesia; it was only that, for a moment, coming into this lane of familiar houses, the things of my life—my name, my parents, my siblings, my sports, my friends, my pastimes—became detached from me; it was as if I could see them at a distance. It was a wonderful moment. I thought to myself, If I am not those things, what am I? And I knew at once that I was the one who was driving this car, and that I was the one thinking these thoughts—that I was something more than the sum of my parts. For that moment, I was afraid of nothing, because I knew I would survive even when the details of my life had faded away.

By the time I reached the house, with the lights in the windows and my father in the garden, my life had already reclaimed me.

In September, the nights were cool and the leaves on the trees began to turn color. At school, it was talk of exams and college visits to the Big Ten. (On a trip to the University of Illinois, I slept in a frat house, saw strippers, watched college football, and vomited.) Every Saturday morning, I went to a prep class for the SATs, a big play late in the game to make up for years of bad grades. The class, in a humdrum brick house in Northfield, was taught by a high school English teacher who had retired to tend to the needs of her husband, Ernie. Two hours into each session, we would hear a yawn and a belch. A moment later, the man himself would emerge in his bathrobe.

He would say, "You kids getting any smarter?"

We took a break while our teacher cooked some eggs for Ernie.

The class was taught around the dining room table, and after the break we made room for Ernie, who, as he ate, watched us as you watch a TV game show, calling out the answers. He argued over the meaning of antonyms and synonyms, shouting, "Bullshit! I call bullshit!"

Jamie met me after each class, or else he was waiting back at my house, watching my father watch football. We would then head to the attic, where we listened to music and he asked what I had learned in class. For the first time, I began to feel a strain between Jamie and myself. It was as if our futures were taking hold of us. He did not have the grades or the money for the colleges where most of our friends would apply. He had only himself. I, on the other hand, had a father and a mother who were busily charting and scheming my next step. On occasion, I felt like one of those trees my father planted in his garden, a fragile tree, like the pink flowering dogwood, that the books said would not survive the northern wind; a tree that, by sheer force of will, my father had brought to bloom.

When I asked my father why he was going to such trouble, he spoke of the world and how it is organized into tracks, inside and outside. Get on the inside track, he said, and there's less distance to travel. On the inside track, you will find jobs and homes and upward mobility. On the outside track, you will cover more ground but still not get as far. My father was not one of those fathers who spoke of hard work as its own reward. History and his own experience had taught him that the world is often run on connections and that, in such a world, the best you can do is be on the inside of those connections. Jamie had no such sense of the world and no one to teach him. So side by side we walked into meetings with halfwit guidance counselors, but we carried ourselves quite differently. I was looking to the years ahead with trepidation but also hope. Jamie did not talk of the future, or of college, though he said he would find somewhere to go. He was simply enjoying his last months of high school, untouched by the ups and downs and heartbreaks of his own past, living in a pocket cut by his style and gestures. If questioned, he would say, "I'm taking it, little brother, one heartbeat at a time."

We took the SATs on a Saturday in October. "This test will be the end of me," said Jamie. In a room on the second floor of our school, I checked the tips of my pencils. Very sharp. In that moment, I had a vision of kids all across America crowding into high schools, sitting at desks, checking pencil points, passing back exams, and waiting for the proctor to say, "Ready, begin!" And then the heart-pounding moment when you turn over the sheet and spot that forest of empty circles. I recognized myself as part of a generation, a nationwide collection of kids, each the product of the same songs and jokes, each facing something like the same future. We were the kids who grew up after disco, which taught us, even more than communism, to fear big ideas.

I could hear the pencil scratches of students getting ahead. Boys and girls at desks, heads down. In a flash, I glimpsed the Reaper moving among them, cutting down the chaff, saving many for lives of quiet desperation, selecting a precious few for summer homes and private jets. I thought, These bastards are out to get me! Take my spot, go to my college, be loved by my parents. I believed I was at last seeing the real world. But just then I spotted Jamie, dark-eyed and grinning as he filled in the boxes. He looked up at me and shrugged. I smiled, read the first question, and in a moment was just another kid at another desk in America.

After the exam, a bunch of us drove to Sloppy Ed's. The hamburger stand stood at the end of a damp street, the windows steamed over. Inside, the air was humid and warm. Ed was behind the counter, his thick hands buried in his apron. He had a tough old-world face. Whenever I saw him, I heard accordions. "You took that test today," he said. "So I'm feeding you for free."

I asked why.

He said, "Oh, because I hate crap like that."

We ate at the counter as Sloppy Ed told us lies about his days in the navy, fighting in 'Nam, and his stint as a circus strongman, about alligator wrestling and how to tell a real blond from a fake: "Look at the mother." Then we went outside to watch the sunset. In Illinois, night comes on slowly, the sun dying into the fields, light on the horizon separating like the contents of an unstirred cocktail. Jamie said, "See it now, because when it goes, it's gone."

Weeks went by, each day shorter than the day before. Our tests were off wherever ungraded tests go. For the moment, the future left us to settle back into our old lives. In November came the first mornings of frost, each blade of grass glistening with ice and casting a shadow. One day, the sky filled with clouds and gusts rattled the windows and the first flakes of snow fell onto the fields. Everything looked strange in the snow, the branches of the big trees weighted down, front yards as crusty as birthday cakes. After school, we stood in the road, fishing for rides. Creeping up behind an idling car, we would take hold of a bumper, bend our knees and skitch off through the slush. A well-chosen truck might carry you for over a mile. It was like flying. When we got home, our faces were wind-burned and we drank hot chocolate or stole sips from the whiskey bottles my parents received as gifts but hardly ever drank. Sometimes we ducked into the shed behind the house and smoked a joint, the acrid smoke hanging in the cold air. Then, filled with profound thoughts, we stretched out before the living room fireplace and watched our shadows dance. Jamie said, "This summer, after school, I think I'll just take off. We live in this great big country, so why settle for this flat little corner of it?"

The winter went that way. I do not remember much else about the days except that they were very cold and we had to wear many layers of clothes and sometimes my hair froze stiffly on my head. By March, the snow turned gray along the roads, and walking in the fields your boots broke through the crusts of ice, and at night the windows filled up with your own reflection, pale and sickly in the dead months of static electricity and random shocks. Winter in Chicago is dark and lonely, and we survived it by going to house parties and studying calendars, imagining the solstice swinging toward us in the night. Then one day it was not so cold, and the next day was even warmer, and the snow turned soupy by afternoon and we were certain that spring was coming. As we walked in the streets of town, the sound of snow melt was everywhere. Jamie said, "With my help, you will now find a girlfriend."

Over the next several weeks, Jamie set up double dates with every kind of girl at school—smart girls and not-so-smart girls, stoned-out girls and girls bound for Harvard or Yale, marching-band girls and girls with nothing much going at all—a plethora, a poo-poo platter, a buffet of nights that began with Jamie racing from his house in some new outfit: linen pants, leather jacket, a cotton shirt with the sleeves rolled, leather shoes, a fisherman's cap, pointy black cowboy boots. And then we were off to Highwood or Lake Forest, girls peeking out from a living room window.

In a sense, it was the same night again and again, with only a change in backdrop—Beinlich's on the highway, where we ate cheeseburgers and apple pie; the second-run dollar-a-pop movie theater in Highland Park, where we watched *Lost in America,* three times; Sam and Hy's in Skokie, dreary old Jewish Skokie, for my all-time favorite, a root-beer float, a scoop of vanilla ice cream melting into its own foam; or just flying through those sleepy little towns that spill down to the dark water of the lake. In the rearview, Jamie whispered to his girl as the split-levels and convenience stores tumbled by.

And later, walking the girl to her door, or along the shore of the secret beach, and the strange sensation of a hand resting in my own, sometimes dry, sometimes damp, the perfume, kissing or being kissed. (It was a great surprise that a girl would let me kiss her, as it would later be an even greater surprise that a girl would let me sleep with her. I still believe it's only convention that convinces a girl to sleep with a boy. After making love, or what on *The Newlywed Game* they used to call whoopee—"Where is the strangest place you and your wife ever made whoopee?"—I would sometimes hug a girl and say, "Thank you, thank you. That is the nicest thing anyone has ever let me do!") Then the drive home, tipsy and reeling. If I was stoned, Jamie would set the cruise control to prevent me from slowing to a crawl. Halfway down my street, I would flick off the headlights and drift into the driveway. We would then sneak up to the attic, climb into the twin beds, and go over the night scene by scene, Jamie giving advice.

Here is what he told me: Greet girls with a broad smile; be engaged at the beginning, indifferent at the end; never be too nice to the parents; talk sometimes about poetry, sometimes about fights; be friendly to the loneliest kid in school because the loneliest kid in school needs friends; now and then, when you are out having fun, ask yourself, "What is Ronnie doing tonight?" Be humble in the knowledge that Ronnie is doing nothing, or else he is in his basement lifting weights, which Jamie called "heavy things in no need of lifting." One night, Jamie, reaching across the space between the beds, touched my arm and said, "Here is the most important thing—do not work too hard. Sit back and let people paint themselves onto you. Don't fight it. Let them see in you whatever they want to see. Let them do the work."

I found myself slipping into a new vocabulary, which I spoke with a clubby ease: Jamie and I talked of prospects, scores, dry spells, long stretches in which you could not find a date, nothing on the plate, nothing on the horizon. Once, when Jamie was in the midst of such a dry spell, he told me he had had a wet dream, which he called a rain dance; he said a rain dance is brought by the rain god, the sweetest and most charitable god of all. Jamie was teaching me a way of life, a habit of moving from girl to girl, never leaving the old girl without a new girl in the wings—each new girl the next hold on the jungle gym, carrying you higher. With each new girl, I could again tell my favorite stories and execute my favorite tricks; with each new girl, I could again see myself reflected as if for the first time; with each new girl, I could again showcase only my best qualities. If I failed and the many bad qualities were showcased accidentally, I could simply switch girls. Each new girl had the power to mint me like a coin.

One night, Jamie and I took our dates to Greek Town. For the kids on the North Shore, Greek Town was Shanghai before the Revolution, or Hot Springs, Arkansas, before Repeal, or Paris between the Wars. It was the port dreamed of by long-haul sailors, a haven of vice. Just off the highway and just west of the Loop, it was a tumbledown strip of seedy immigrant dives. Each restaurant had the same menu of overstewed beef and cheap red wine served by waiters in dinner jackets. There was Santorini and The Greek Isles and half a dozen other joints, but our favorite was Diana's. Driving my parents' car, I picked up Jamie and the girls, got on the highway, and did my best to keep quiet. I did not laugh or smile. If I had to say something—"If we don't get gas, the night is ruined"—I made sure it was gloomy.

I had been set up with Heather Blunt, a serious-minded blond girl with long legs, green eyes, good grades, and smart friends. I had had a crush on Heather since sophomore year, when we shared a lab table in biology. The teacher, a kindly old white-haired gentleman, had opened the class by saying, "Over break, I had heart valve surgery, so I may die at any time; let's begin." In class, I made many smart-ass remarks and talked back to the movies (*Why Planet Earth? Zinc and You!*) that ran before us like propaganda. Sometimes, with my safety goggles in place, I caused the Bunsen burners to spark up like factory vents.

Two years later, when I set my mind on a date with Heather and so sent word through that network of high school girls that is even more effective than the pneumatic tubes that once carried messages to the far-flung corners of vast office buildings, word shot back: Heather says no; she is afraid a date with you will play like a sitcom. "You're too much of a clown," Pistone explained. "She thinks, in the middle of messing around, you'll stop to make some dumb joke."

It was a crushing response and certainly true, so I took it to heart. Even years later I still believed a person could be either serious or funny but never both. I thought any joke you told, no matter how well-turned, would shoot holes in the serious impression you might be trying to make. After that, whenever I saw Heather at school, I frowned and spoke of continental drift, of nuclear war, of my general sense of dread. I often used the phrase "To hell in a handbasket" or said "It will get worse before it gets to worse." One day, when Heather mentioned a millionaire who had been caught bilking other millionaires, I said, "It is easier for a camel to pass through the eye of a needle than it is for a rich man to enter the kingdom of God." The next day, Heather agreed to go on a date with me. In the car, I did my best to stay in character—a serious young man weighed down by the problems of the world. When Jamie asked if I had seen David Letterman the night before, I said, "I do not watch that kind of television."

He said, "What kind of television do you watch?"

I said, "Public television."

A few minutes later, when Jamie asked what I thought of the new Tom Petty record, I said, "When you consider the fact that, at any moment, whether by design or by some absurd accident, we might well die in a fiery conflagration, does Tom Petty really matter?"

I found a parking spot in front of Diana's. The sun had gone down. The sky was that cool shade of blue often used as a background in passport photos. Jamie said, "C'mon, little brother, let's get a table."

We found a booth in back of the restaurant. We ordered a bottle of red wine. The waiter asked if we were twenty-one.

Jamie said, "Sir, I will kindly ask you not to insult me or my friends."

The waiter shrugged and came back with a bottle. And soon we were eating stringy meat and fried bread from silver platters. The room was filled with chattering voices, singing, and dishes breaking as waiters shouted *"Opa!"* and set fire to plates of cheese. We finished the bottle and ordered another. With each glass, the floor, which was made of that kind of black-and-white checkered tile you see in old Italian kitchens, danced and shimmered before my eyes. On the way to the bathroom, to steady myself, I had to look at my shoes. I said, "I am buzzed, I am loaded, I am drunk." It seemed exciting and dangerous as slowly, drink by drink, Heather opened up like a flower, sitting close and holding my hand as I said, "See how serious I am? Serious, serious motherfucker. Like Kissinger I am so serious."

From there, my memory is a blocked station on cable, an occasional image flickering through the static: Jamie leading me to the car and taking away my keys; me sitting in back with Heather, kissing Heather, saying, "I love you, I love you, I love you"; highway signs spinning past like lemons in a slot machine; my stomach turning over and me shouting, "Pull over!" I ran into the trees and puked into the Skokie lagoon, that lonesome swamp where the mob dumps its bodies. We must have dropped off the girls, because the next thing I knew Jamie and I were in the front hall of my house, looking up the stairs, where my mother, in a sheer nightgown, stood on the landing, eyes clouded with sleep, saying, "Honey, is that you? Are you home?"

I felt the bile rise inside me and rushed into the bathroom. I could hear my mother repeat her question—"Honey, is that you? Are you home?"—and the instant before I started to panic, before I thought, All is lost, I heard Jamie's voice, slow and steady, say, "Yes, I am home."

My mother said, "Good night, honey, I love you."

And, in a response that even then I registered as symbolic, Jamie said, "Good night, Mom. I love you too."

In April, we went to a party thrown by Rink Anderson, a handsome kid with a broad smile and a cool reserve I recognized from sixties movies about surfing. Rink was the big blond kid on the periphery. His speech was wide-open and breezy and sprinkled with trademark phrases. If, for example, a party went south, he said, "Let's bail." If a friend smoked some bad dope and started to panic, he said, "Take a breath and ride down the crest." If you got dumped by your girlfriend, he said, "You will always have country music."

Rink was a strange hybrid, a sweet and melancholy popular kid. In junior high, after years of being the coolest kid in grade school, Rink gained a bunch of weight, his prepubescent body fueling up for the blastoff that would carry it above six feet; for a time, he was ridiculed by the very kids who had once worshiped him. In high school, when Rink resumed his place atop the social order, he cherished the memory of his chubby years; in the story of Rink Anderson, I've always felt his brief stint as a fat kid played a role similar to the role polio played in the life of FDR—it gave him depth; it gave him empathy with the masses.

The Andersons lived in the kind of house you might see in an Alfred Hitchcock movie, a marble slab built into the side of a ravine overhanging the lake. Every window was filled with water and sky. We stood on the back porch as night crept across the waves. Rink had the radio tuned to a weekly show called *Blues Breakers*. He hummed along with Sonny Boy Williamson. Every few minutes, the doorbell rang and another group of kids came in. When it got dark, Jamie and I went to the living room, where I saw the kind of cute little blond girl that has always made my heart fly into my mouth. She was talking to friends, and now and then she looked over at me. Jamie saw me looking at her, went over, and introduced himself. I went into the kitchen. When I got back, Jamie said, "I have it all worked out."

Jamie arranged it so the girl and I were left alone on the back porch. As I looked at her, I wondered what my face was doing. She smiled. She said her name was Molly. We went into a back room and sat on a bed in the dark. There were other couples on other beds. After a while, we walked down to the beach. We talked. I said something romantic. I drove her home. A few nights later, we went on a date with Jamie and a friend of Molly's. Then we went out alone. Then she was my girlfriend.

Molly was just another suburban girl with a room full of stuffed animals and snapshots, but to me she was a Gypsy from the steppes, wild and exotic. I came to know her secrets and to fill in the gaps of her stories. In her place, I built a figure of romance, standing in a fog at the end of the platform. My brother, home from college, said, "I did not know they made human beings that white." Pistone said, "Like so many nice girls, she is plain." Jamie thought of her as a starter kit, a demo to introduce me to the toggles and joysticks. Still, she was my girlfriend, and for this reason alone I cherished her and cared about her.

We met during free periods in the student commons. Around my friends, she was shy. She would nod and blush and look away. But after school, when we were alone, she burned with a low fever, saying my name, guiding my hand. Since I had no experience of sex, I found my way by trial and error, hoping to inflict as little pain as possible. Looking for the sweet spot, we rubbed each other raw. On spring nights, we worked our way from stage to stage— from kissing and squeezing, to undoing and unclasping, to holding and stroking. We fooled around in her bedroom when her parents were at dinner, in my bedroom when my parents were out of town, at the houses of friends, in wood-paneled family rooms in the flickering light of rented movies—*Stripes, Volunteers.* We did not have sex, but instead lived in the gray land of the dry hump and the hand job, where your mind is capable of imagining nothing grander than the blow job, the great mystical blow job that stands as the crowning jewel of any truly worthy high school relationship.

One night, in the attic, with the windows open to the cool breeze, with Bo Diddley on the stereo shouting his fast, dirty version of "My Babe"— "My babe, when she gets hot, she gets hot like an oven"—I was crowned, brought from the shallows of boyhood into the wavery depths; and all the while, my parents just downstairs watching *Dynasty*. After I dropped Molly off at home, I went into their room. My father asked me about colleges. As I answered his questions, part of me marveled: The fool! How he talks! As if I am the same boy that he knew this morning!

When Jamie told me he would not go to the senior prom, I said I would not go either. The truth is, I had already begun to tire of Molly. In those weeks, I had time only for myself—my own worries, the riddle of my own future. Each day, a few more kids came to school waving envelopes, saying they had been accepted by the college of their choice, second choice, safety; and just like that, they were relieved, for another four years anyway, of the dread fact of having no idea what to do.

You see, for the most part, the kids I grew up with had been taught that being a success means doing better than your parents, and that doing better than your parents means making more money—but our parents were rich. So what chance did we have of making more money, and why should we want to? What mattered to our parents could never matter to us. What mattered to us—a sense of style, of experience-collecting—seemed so simple and pure we were afraid even to talk about it.

As a result, most of the kids in towns like Glencoe and Winnetka just went along, high school to college to whatever, hoping they might someday, as if by magic, understand the longing of their fathers, who themselves had made a mistake known to successful fathers throughout history—they had raised rich kids. For the kids on the North Shore this meant seeing college as a hack politician sees another term—four more years, a reprieve, an escape—as it would later mean trying to lose their inheritance in one grand post-college spree, or indeed trying to make even more money than their parents, or trying to spend more, or devising some entirely new notion of success. Of course, to a degree, Jamie and I were immune from such concerns. My father and mother were in no way conventional, and Jamie's father was not even in the picture. Still, this was the world where we grew up, and it marked us. As we got older, we became increasingly interested in the idea of success and in how to make our way, without too much injury, into the thicket of the adult world.

One by one, my friends caught the reprieve—Tom

Pistone to Illinois State University at Normal, Tyler White to Michigan State University at Lansing, Rink Anderson to the University of Montana at Missoula, Ronnie Flowers to the University of Iowa at Iowa City, where, though he could start over, he would still be Ronnie Flowers. In addition to an acceptance letter, Ronnie had also landed himself Casey Cassidy, a girl he met at the health club, a female Ronnie, choppy red hair, scattershot, hopeful. Ronnie drove Casey's car as if it were his own—a green Jaguar. Once, when Jamie and I were in the car, a phone rang and Ronnie answered it, saying, "Yes, Casey. . . . No, Casey. . . . Of course, Casey. . . . I love you, Casey."

A few days later, my father asked to speak to Ronnie alone. He began by asking about Casey: "Where is she from? What does her father do? Does she have a sister? Is she nice? How many miles are on that Jaguar? How does it handle? What does her house look like on the inside?" After Ronnie had answered each of these questions, my father said, "Ronnie, you know I care about you, right? I want only what is in your best interest? You know that I am thinking only of you?"

"Yes, Herbie."

"Good, Ronnie. Because I don't want you to take this in the wrong way. Ronnie, marry that girl! Marry her now while you still have the chance. You will never do better, Ronnie. And this is no insult. Believe me, if she had a sister, which, sadly, she does not, I would urge Richard to marry the sister."

. . .

In May, I was accepted to Tulane University in New Orleans. My parents were not home when the letter came, so I went down the street to tell Ronnie. His mother, Chris Flowers, who was baking cookies, said, "Oh, really? I went to Tulane."

At the same moment, in unison, Ronnie and I said, "You did?"

"For a year," said Chris. "Then I dropped out."

Again in unison, Ronnie and I said, "You dropped out?"

"Yes," said Chris. "To get married to my first husband, the one before Bob."

From there, Ronnie was on his own.

He said, "You were married before you were married to Dad?"

Ronnie asked some more questions and then dropped the subject. He actually seemed to lose interest. That is the amazing thing about Ronnie—his inability to wonder, to worry, to suffer. As I got older, I realized this would be his ticket to true happiness. Ronnie Flowers is a kid who gets hit in the head with a baseball bat, but the moment before he gets hit is still the greatest moment of his life.

When I told Jamie my news, the results were far less gothic. He smiled and shook my hand and said he would now have a reason to visit the South. "It will be like we're still together," he said. When I asked if he had heard from any schools, he told me that, come to think of it, he had not applied to any. In the past, if questioned, Jamie had always spoken in a vague way of the university in Indiana or Wisconsin, and I guess I had assumed he had applied to some of the big state schools. Now I didn't know what he would do.

Some weeks later, Jamie and my father were working in our garden: Jamie in shorts, no shirt, dirt-smeared; my father like a cavalry officer in an old war movie: High Plains drifter hat, stubbly beard, cigar. A pilgrim and a wild Indian talking on the naked prairie.

"What is this about you not going to college?"

"Didn't say not going. Just didn't apply. Up in the air. Figure to figure."

"The world is full of morons, Jamie. Don't be one of them. Mistakes you make now, these are real mistakes."

"I'm just taking my time."

"Is this about money?"

"No, it has nothing to do with money."

"Because if it does I can help. I'll pay your tuition. I don't want you to make a stupid mistake."

"Don't worry," said Jamie. "I'll be fine."

In June, the *New Trier News,* for which, on occasion, I still wrote, ran a list of the colleges that each senior would attend. Taken together with your class rank, this list was thought to tell the entire story of your life. In the paper, next to Jamie's name, there was an empty space. When I thought of it later, Jamie's decision not to apply seemed brave. He was the only kid I knew with the personality to face that spring without an acceptance letter. You see, in those weeks, I had a sense that life after graduation was already beginning to claim my classmates, that the kids in school were being defined by their future. Pistone walked the halls with shoulders slumped, as if every passing hour brought him closer to his unpleasant fate—Bucko, fallen idol of my father's youth, was calling. Pistone, at least, went easy, without much fuss or complaint. Other kids— and here I am thinking of a big kid named Will Tickle— had to be dragged kicking and screaming from their glory. Will peaked freshman year. He went downhill from there. By senior year, he no longer had success with girls, or sports, or friends. He seemed to sense that the world outside of school would be even more cruel. He was like a stock that gets devalued and devalued until one day it just drops off the big board.

The future wanted to define Jamie too—people could not look at him without seeing that empty space next to his name—but he would not let it. To him, the coming years were a trap he would find his way out of. He walked the halls with confidence, a plain sentence in fancy script, a bird puffed up with air. He wanted only a life free of other people's dreams, open to the sensations of a greater world.

One afternoon, as I sat in Earth Science, a class every- one called Rocks for Jocks, and I looked at Ronnie—who, due to the mockeries of fate, shared my lab table—Jamie appeared in the doorway in jeans and the sort of colorful shirt Sammy Davis Jr. wore in his prime. When the teacher turned to the blackboard, I ducked into the hall, and Ronnie followed.

Blues Fest was being held downtown at Grant Park. Jamie unfolded a schedule of the festival and said, "Melvin Taylor is playing. Let's go."

"How can we just go?" asked Ronnie.

"Easy," said Jamie. "We drive."

We met Pistone in the commons and ducked out the back door. There was a shaggy-haired school official in the parking lot, a narc in a Members Only jacket, and as we climbed into Tom's car he shouted at us, but Jamie turned up the radio and gunned the engine out onto the main road. We followed the lake past the big coast mansions. It was a thrill driving away from school, the red-brick behemoth fading in the rearview mirror.

Tom put the top down. The sun beat on my arms. Jamie smiled at me and said, "We must all do as the Buddhists do and live in the now—in the great glorious here and now." For Jamie, this was, of course, a joke. He was making fun of all that New Age garbage we watched on late-night TV, but doing so in a way that said, Hold on, maybe there is something of use here. However, realizing that, since our minds were always racing ahead, it was impossible for people like us to actually live in the now ("For one thing," he said, "not one of us has the right clothes"), he decided we should instead be satisfied to live in the five-minutes-from-now. "Keep your mind tuned to the moment just beyond this moment," he said, smiling, "and that is where you will live, and that is where I will look for you."

When we reached Chicago, it was windswept and golden. We stood at the foot of the John Hancock tower. It is almost a hundred stories tall. It goes up and up. If you look up too long, it makes you dizzy.

When we got to Grant Park, Tom, using his fake ID, bought drinks. We walked from stage to stage, sipping foam. The city, following the curve of the shore, rose and fell like the notes on a music staff. The water stretched to the horizon, as cool and clean as a sheet of marble.

Melvin Taylor came on at 3 p.m. We stood in the crowd, watching his fingers move up and down the neck of his guitar. Jamie was at my side. "This is my music," he said. "It makes me feel like swaggering." Then he was gone. A moment later, he was up on the stage—I still don't know how this happened—dancing with one of the backup singers.

Tom said, "He's not bad."

Later on, we stood under the trees, thumping Jamie on the back, saying, "Fuck college, just dance."

It was getting to be late afternoon, and behind us someone set off a bottle rocket. It climbed into the sky and then it sputtered and fell into the lake. We stood at the edge of the crowd, listening to horns and guitars, the cries of a singer. It was sad and not sad. In daylight, you always have a much sharper sense of what you are leaving behind.

I graduated from high school on a Wednesday night in June. The boys wore tuxedo pants and white dinner jackets and moved with the grace of lounge singers. Since there were a thousand kids in my class, the ceremony was divided into two sessions. Heading into the gym for the late session, I ran into Jamie, who was coming from the early session. He had already graduated and was being fussed over by his mother and grandmother. Isn't it funny how people still make such a big deal out of a high school graduation? Pulling me aside, he said, "See how it works? With all your plans and even that acceptance letter riding in your pocket, it is me who graduates first. If the world ends right now—and don't laugh, because the Bible is full of shit like that—I get the degree and you get nothing!"

He opened his jacket and showed me the flask tucked inside. "When you're out, grab Molly and meet me down at Ming Lee."

A few hours later, when we got to the lake, Jamie was on the shore, a bottle in his hand, a cigarette dangling from his mouth. Smoke hung in his wake and he had an arm around Allison Drake, a girl he had been dating for maybe two weeks. He shook my hand. Allison laughed. Allison laughed all the time, but really she had one of the saddest faces I have ever seen—a long upper lip, high cheekbones, murky green eyes. Her brother was a few years older than us, owned a hearse, and drove it around with the windows open, blasting The Dead Kennedys. One night, Allison borrowed the hearse and parked it behind her church. She and Jamie had sex in back where they put the coffins. In the morning, when the Methodists of Winnetka turned up in their Sunday clothes to pray, Jamie was exhilarated. "So you know what I did," he said. "I went in and I prayed right along with them—only I was different. God was up there winking at me, saying, 'There you go, boy, go forth and multiply!' "

We built a fire on the beach and passed around a bottle of cheap wine. The night turned cold and there were whitecaps on the dark water. I do not remember what Jamie and I talked about, but I think we were very happy and spoke of our friendship and how it would go on and on. This was the age of irony, and people dared not show genuine affection. Between expressions of love, we would dismiss it all with a wave of the hand or say something like "Don't go fag on me." Now and then, I looked across the fire at Molly. We had been running downhill since I did not ask her to that big dance. I had decided to break up with her in the morning. And I missed her already. When I told Jamie, he said, "Ever notice how, whichever direction you walk, you're walking away?"

An incident later that night delayed my plans. As Molly and I settled on a blanket near the fire, a strange warmth climbed up my legs. I felt sleepy and started to doze off, but Molly shouted, "You're on fire! You're on fire!" I jumped. The blanket was in flames and so were the cheap pants of my rented tuxedo. I danced down the beach hollering like Richard Pryor. Jamie coughed out the stink of burning polyester. Then, just as I accepted my long future in the burn ward, Molly knocked me down and buried me in sand. In other words, she put me out. How can you break up with a girl who has put you out? So instead we just kept on dating until it was clear to both of us that our fling had lost its flavor; it had been chewed out like gum. A few years later, I heard that Molly had fallen in with the football players and had even gone downtown to Rizzo's to play the game. But by then I no longer cared.

Just before dawn, Jamie and I went for a swim. It is exhilarating to go swimming in the dark with the moon on the water. Past the pier, we turned and looked back at the shore. Jamie said, "You want to hear my plan? I call it Reach the Beach. I'll hitchhike west, not stopping until the road ends, and I'll swim in the ocean, which I've never seen, and the salt water will wash me clean. And on the way I'll see some of America, and to tell you the truth I'm thinking of it as a kind of baptism, a second baptism, but this one I'll give to myself."

He then explained how, growing up in Illinois, we were buffeted, in every direction, by a thousand miles of rest stops. "It's a part of our identity," he said, "being the kids in the middle—in the middle of the country, in the middle of the road, in the middle of nothing." By swimming in the sea, he hoped to return, in time for the last big summer parties, as a man of western sunsets and western skies. That is what he told me, anyway, and I admired him for it.

A few days later, I went to Jamie's house and watched him pack. Shirts and pants stuffed in a duffel bag. Every few minutes, his grandmother poked her face in the door and said, "Why, Jamie?"

On our way out, his mother said, "You do not know the first thing about it, and you have no idea of the coldness you will meet."

In the car, I asked Jamie what his mother had been talking about.

He said, "Not even she knows."

I drove out to the expressway and dropped him near the on-ramp. He promised to call and write, keeping me informed of every adventure. Then I watched him scramble down the embankment onto the shoulder of the road. He was wearing jeans and a faded work shirt. He stuck out his thumb, and in a few minutes an eighteen-wheeler pulled over. Jamie threw his bag on his shoulder and ran for it, climbing into the cab, and a moment later he was gone.

That summer, while Jamie was away, some friends and I organized a softball team to play in the local gasoline league. As the name suggests, many of the teams were

sponsored by filling stations—Jean's 76 was a dynasty—
and were fleshed out by rough boys who spent their days
under the hoods of cars. These were big fellas from the
west suburbs, several years older than us, with greasy fingers and thick torsos. My friends and I were still smooth-
faced, slender-hipped boys. Since the games could get
rough, we only recruited kids we knew could play—high
school athletes in search of a summer fling. We practiced
on a field behind our old junior high, a rocky expanse a
few blocks from town. Sometimes a group of girls would
watch us practice. After driving a ball or making a
highlight-film grab, you would turn and smile at the girls.

In my mind I can still run down the roster of our team,
just as many Chicagoans can name the entire '69 Cubs. At
first base was Reed Cole, a big bear of a kid with a wide
back and an ambling, doe-dee-doe-here-I-go walk. At
second base was Tyler White, who later became a com-
mercial prop pilot out of a regional airport that was
described to me as "The O'Hare of northern Wisconsin."
At shortstop was Jordie McQuaid, who, when buying a
pair of running shoes, told the saleslady, "I don't care
about all that shit, just tell me, Do they look cool?" On the
bench during a hockey game, McQuaid once said, "After
that goal, I could've had any girl in the stands, including
the mothers." At third base was Tom Pistone, who played
in a daredevil style that featured many head-first slides. I
played left field. In center field was Chick Young, whose

face was as neatly cut as a copper penny. Rink Anderson was in right field. Our pitcher was a wannabe fire spotter who actually pulled off a pickoff play that requires the first baseman to hide the ball under his shirt. The catcher was whoever we could pick up at the last minute. On the bench to fill out the roster was Ronnie Flowers.

We called our team the North Shore Screen Doors. To us, the screen door was a lyrical symbol of summer. We had jerseys made up that showed a screen door with wide eyes and a spooky smile. On the backs were our nicknames. For myself I chose the nickname Desoto Andujar, which sounded (to me) like a Dominican prospect not quite good enough for the major leagues. This was the year of the Super Bowl Shuffle, so we even wrote up a little song to make clear our intentions: "We ain't out there just to get a tan,/we're out there doin' the screen door slam!" On a schedule, however, the name read like just another one of the industrial concerns that played in the league: Wilmette Tread & Tire, Gary's Sunoco, North Shore Screen Doors. As a result, upon first spotting us, opposition players always burst out laughing: "Look at these pretty boys from the North Shore! We'll slaughter 'em!" Most of the games were played after dinner on a field at the edge of Glencoe under floodlights that could be seen across town. On a good night, a few hundred people packed into the rickety bleachers and followed the action on the hand-turned scoreboard. Beyond the lights was a stretch of oak trees. Train tracks ran through the trees, and now and then you could hear the whistle and see the light of the engine playing across the trunks.

Before games, as we took batting practice, Tom and I talked about Drew-licious. He had promised to write long description-filled letters, but I had heard almost nothing from him. One night, he had telephoned—a collect call from a bar, dead drunk, proclaiming the beauty of everything. Another time, he called collect and said he was in Las Vegas and a cocktail waitress was hot for him but he was too drunk to know how to proceed. I told him to write his room number on a napkin. It seemed like something Wayne Newton might do. Jamie said, "Yeah, yeah," and hung up. Tom showed up to one game with a postcard, a few salutations scribbled on the back of a picture of Dinosaur Park. And that was it.

"Where do you think he is right now?" I asked.

"I bet he is walking down the road with his pack," said Tom. "I bet it is hot as hell and he is parched and hoping for a ride."

"Does he get one?"

"Hell, yes, here comes a pickup truck loaded with girls."

The Screen Doors had gotten off to a rabbit start, winning four games in the first three weeks. It was a real pleasure to beat up on these big brawlers from behind the pumps. I still have a clear memory of Jordie McQuaid fielding a ball with a neat stutter step and flipping it to first base with a sidearm; of Tom Pistone tearing around third and diving into home plate in a cloud of dirt; of Ronnie Flowers reaching for a water bottle and spilling Gatorade across his gut. After each game we went out celebrating.

The summer before college was a summer of parties, cars parked up and down side streets, kids passed out in back lawns, sneaking with girls into locked master bedrooms, swiping booze from locked liquor cabinets, getting stoned in basements finished and unfinished, climbing chain-link fences, pool hopping, splashy cannonballs, and cops. Beer was a constant at these parties, sloshing in kegs, foaming in cups, turning the heads of beautiful girls who went dancing off into the lake. Beer, whatever we could get, Mickey's or Pabst or Schlitz, pervaded each night like a dirty wind. The big song on the radio, much to our national shame, was "Wang Chung," with the endlessly recurring chorus: "Everyone have fun tonight! Everyone Wang Chung tonight!" Before I took a slug, a friend would warn, "If you plan to Wang Chung tonight, please don't drive!" Staggering to his feet, raising his cup, Pistone said, "Toast with me. To our friend Drew-licious, who at this moment is stepping across the Continental Divide."

In July, the Screen Doors began to lose, sometimes in back-and-forth down-to-the-wire nail-biters, sometimes in blowouts. On occasion, the slaughter rule had to be invoked. I was the captain of the team. I responded by juggling the lineup, bringing beer to practice, banning beer from practice. Nothing worked. As we lost to filling stations from up and down the turnpike, as the wind carried each ball over our heads, as squalls from the east stalled each rally, I felt like the Fisher King of myth, suffering through a season of drought. To lose like this, week after week, seemed the worst kind of bad luck. When all else failed, I spoke to my father, who knew everything about baseball. He promised to come to our next practice.

He walked over from town, cigar in his mouth. He leaned against the backstop and watched us field and hit. His eyes followed the play. He made notes on a yellow legal pad. At the end of practice, he told me we were undisciplined, stupid, reckless. "Can I help you?" he said. "Yes, I can. But you must do exactly as I say. I will not have two coaches of this team."

In those days, my father looked a great deal like Walter Matthau, a fact often commented on by minor acquaintances and strangers. For these people, my father was touched by the mystery of that minor deity, the celebrity look-alike. On a flight to Roanoke, West Virginia, he overheard a couple arguing across the aisle, the woman saying, "No, it's not him."

"It certainly is him," said the man.

"Then why is he flying coach?"

"How should I know? Maybe he's researching a role."

To prove his point, the man then shouted, "Walter! Walter! Walter!"

It was this resemblance—the same jowls, fleshy face,

high forehead, grand nose, humorous eyes—that convinced my friends to accept my father as their leader. Since Walter Matthau made such an excellent coach in *The Bad News Bears*, a movie we had grown up with and still loved, it was decided that Herbie could lead the Screen Doors back to glory. Before his first game, we gave him a jersey that said BOILERMAKER, Matthau's nickname in the film. Of course, it was a kind of joke, but my father took it quite seriously. At the next practice, he made us run wind sprints. "It's all about conditioning," he explained. "Late in the game, when those other guys are sucking air, you'll have your legs." There were double-play drills and triple-play drills, and we had to practice hitting to the opposite field. For the most part, my friends just shrugged off these drills. The only person who would do just as my father said was Ronnie Flowers. So my father worked with Ronnie, hitting fungoes, shouting out words of encouragement. "Thatta boy, Ronnie! Now throw, damn you, throw!" When I told my father he was wasting time, that Ronnie would never play in a game, he said, "We will see."

And still, we kept losing. I could tell it was bothering my father. When, after an especially poor performance, he saw some of our players clowning in the parking lot, he said, "Of course they are Cub fans, nobody told them there is nothing good about being bad." My father took a special interest in Tom Pistone, who he said was the best pure athlete on the Screen Doors. By helping Tom was he trying to turn back the clock? Was he trying to save his old pal Bucko? Tom was forever swinging for the fences, driving the ball hundreds of feet, where it died harmlessly in the glove of an outfielder. "So look what you have," my father would say. "You have a long out." He urged Tom to hit the ball on the ground, saying, "You will beat it out every time." Tom followed this advice for a few weeks, smacking balls all over the infield, recording dozens of singles. In the end, however, swayed by the girls in the stands, Tom went back to the long ball. "That is the problem with your generation," said my father. "You each want to do it alone by yourselves, and so you will each fail alone by yourselves."

"Yes," said Jordie McQuaid. "But we will look cool doing it."

My father reached his breaking point at the end of July. He had flown home early from a business trip to make our game against Jean's 76. He dropped his bags at the house and walked over to the field in his business suit and loafers. It was a blustery summer night. The floodlights cut a neat piece of green out of the darkness. Beyond the lights, trees strained in the breeze. Beyond the trees were streets lined with houses. The field was soft and moist, and there was the wonderful smell of cut grass. Now and then, the wind blew dust across the ground. Pistone, at third base, was yelling, "A little pepper, boys! A little pepper!" The bleachers were filled with people from town, some in shorts, some in khakis, and our girls were there, and so were some of the kids we knew from school. Ronnie's father, Bob Flowers, was there and so was Sloppy Ed and the Korean guy who owned Ray's Sports Shop, who shouted, "No shoes? You really need new shoes, huh?"

In the first inning, Jean's 76 collected three quick runs, mostly on drives down the left-field line. When we came up, Tom tried to smack the ball into the trees, then I did the same, and so did Jordie McQuaid. My father shook his head, turned to Ronnie, and said, "Be ready." Jean's tacked on a few runs each inning, until we were on the verge of the slaughter rule. As we ran out for the fifth inning, my father shouted to Tyler White. He told him to move from second base and reposition himself behind the shortstop; the center fielder was to shade into left; the right fielder was to move into center. It was something like the old Ted Williams shift—my father said it would counteract the other team's deadly pull hitting. I said his plan was idiotic and embarrassing. We would not do it. He walked out onto the field and said, "What did I tell you about two coaches?"

He was standing near the pitcher's mound, and soon we were shouting at each other in front of the entire town. The players on the bench for Jean's 76 were laughing. "Desoto Andujar," one of them yelled. "Look at Desoto Andujar!" The umpire threatened to call a delay of game. My father said to me, "You're out! Get on the bench!" He turned to the dugout and called for Ronnie, who raced over like a frisky retriever. My father said, "Ronnie, get into left field."

"Ronnie doesn't play," I said.

"He's playing now," said my father.

From the seats, Bob Flowers shouted, "Go get 'em, Ronnie."

I said, "No."

My father said, "What?"

I said, "You're fired."

My father looked at me, and I could not tell if he was hurt or if he was smiling. Maybe both. He turned and walked out of the lights. He walked home. Ronnie trotted back to the dugout. The next inning, the other team's catcher, a huge fat man, hammered a pitch high into the air. I watched it vanish into the black sky and a moment later I heard it drop into the trees. I had never seen a softball hit that hard. Three runs scored. The slaughter rule was invoked. The season was over.

A few days later, I went by Jamie's house. I told Violet that Jamie had borrowed something of mine, that I knew where it was, and that I needed it back. She held open the door. Of course, this was a lie. I just felt like looking around. I walked out to the porch. Everything was as he left it, his bed neatly made and his books stacked evenly on their shelves. I opened his closet and looked at his pants and at the neat row of shoes and at the neat pile of shirts. I looked at his desk, at the pictures he had set out: his father backed by mountains, the skyline of Chicago, Little Walter in a crisp white suit, blowing his harmonica.

In a drawer, I found a stack of notebooks. I sat down and looked through the pages. These were journals, hundreds of entries, some long paragraphs, some sketchy descriptions of feelings or moods, some just a single phrase or word. The pages were written in the same style as Jamie's speech, with each sentence running on and on, circling toward some greater truth. There were theories and ideas in the notebooks, and notions and descriptions and anecdotes and dreams and predictions and stories. Sloppy Ed Carter was in it, and so was the lake ten minutes after sundown ("the sky red and the water so blue it hurt my eyes"), and Ronnie was in it and so was my father, stumbling through the garden like a High Plains drifter, and I was in it, and so was Tom, raising a beer, and God was there, and so too were about a thousand clocks, each ticking off the hours, and there were short little poems and lists, which read to me like something from the diaries of old Ben Franklin, just another experience-crazed American dead set to reinvent himself, and there were stories, one about a Mexican landscaping crew that worked in the yards up and down the North Shore, their broken-down pickup truck rattling with tools and stink-

ing of manure, "the most wretched, hardworking out-
siders in the world," and in the back of each story was
Jamie's father, ambling the great green pastures of heaven.
On the last page, there was an entry written a week before
Jamie left on his trip:

> I live in the suburbs with my mother and my sister and
> my grandmother, almost a prisoner but full of road
> dreams and the constant anticipation of adventures in
> strange cities. At night, I pore over maps and imagine
> every highway and hill and out of the way town. I
> approach big cities in my mind. I explore every back
> street and alley. From the tops of tall buildings I enjoy
> crystal views of streets spilling into the country.
> Sometimes the streets are filled with traffic and some-
> times they are deserted and I am alone.

As I was reading, Violet came in. I never thought of
myself as a snoop, as someone who looks through closets
and reads the diaries of other people, but then again—
here I was. Violet said, "I have fixed you lunch."

"I can't stay."

I ran through the house and out to my car. I drove
through town and into the fields. I cannot say just how I
was feeling. Like a creep, I guess, empty too. In such
moments, I feel that everything is spinning and everyone
is changing; even the universe is spinning, so the loss of
this moment and this mood and these friends will be so

utterly complete that no one, not even me, will be around
to remember it. I don't know. It's kind of impossible to
explain. I pushed the accelerator to the floor. I love to
speed through the country, flying past cornstalks and telephone poles. Whatever is bothering me, whatever is under
my skin—a pain which, like the houses beyond the horizon, I can sense but not yet see—is blown away, and my
head clears, and my heart races.

One afternoon in August I was sitting at the counter of
Sloppy Ed's, eating a charburger and reading Mike
Royko's column in the *Sun-Times,* when I overheard a conversation between two kids I knew in a vague way—kids
who drifted on the edge of school life, riding skateboards
and hanging out in the smoking area, emerging, like
strange tropical birds, in only the hottest days of summer.
One kid was named Chester, but everyone called him
Chester the Molester, because he had once dropped his
pants and displayed himself to a busload of Catholic
schoolgirls. The other kid was also named Chester, but
everyone called him Chester the Ingestor, because he
would swallow anything. In the course of one summer
afternoon, Chester swallowed two Valiums, a cockroach, a
piece of broken glass, a butterfly, and an entire bottle of
Tylenol. The Chesters were talking as they took turns on
Donkey Kong, a video game that filled the hamburger
stand with a cartoon collection of chirps and beeps.

Here is what they were saying:

Chester the Molester: No way, man, catch it, he is way fucking different. I heard he saw some crazy shit out there and that it *fried* his brain.

Chester the Ingestor: I heard he saw a Swami. Fucking Swami gave him a whole shitload of healing crystals. At the airport, they made him put the fucking crystals through the X-ray machine, and the crystals lost maybe fifty percent of their healing power. Maybe that's what fried him.

Chester the Molester: Bullshit, he hitched back. No. It was the whole fucking thing, man. It did him in! He was gonna Jack Kerouac it out there, swim in the ocean, and Jack Kerouac it back. But something went all screwy.

Chester the Ingestor: I heard he took a medicine cabinet full of pills.

Chester the Molester: I heard he banged a hundred hot chicks.

Chester the Ingestor: Maybe that's what fried him. He has eaten everything on the menu, and now there is nothing left to taste.

Chester the Molester: And he is stuck back here where there is nothing but takeout and skank.

Chester the Ingestor: Hey, you ever make it to the third cartoon on this machine?

I went over and asked who the hell they were talking about. Chester the Ingestor kept his eyes on the video screen. Chester the Molester looked at me.

"What do you mean?" he said. "Drew-licious."

"What? Is he home?"

"Fuck, yeah, he's been home for at least a week."

I did not believe it at first. I thought one or both of the Chesters were lying. Then I did believe it and I was really happy. Jamie is back! Then I still believed it, but I was hurt. Why had Jamie slipped back into town without a word? Why had he ditched me? These were my thoughts as I walked to his house. I found him on the stoop, smoking, looking at the streets of town, his hair swept back, his face tawny. He said, "Hey, little brother, I was wondering when you would show up."

"What the fuck? Why didn't you call me?"

"C'mon," he said. "Don't do the obvious thing and be mad at me."

For a moment, I was actually too mad to say anything. In addition, I felt like a fool for being so obvious in my anger. I said, "Fine. Tell me what I should be?"

"Well, I guess you should just be happy to see me."

I waited a moment, then said, "Yes. I am happy to see you. Welcome home."

Jamie threw open his arms and smiled his great big smile, but it was only his mouth smiling. The rest of his face was gloomy. Despite the fineness of his features, and his broad shoulders, and his clear eyes, he looked washed out, defeated. I asked about his trip and he said, "There is nothing much to talk about." I asked if he had made it to the Pacific Ocean and he said, "Can't you tell? I'm a new man." I asked if he had reached any decision about his immediate future; had he decided on a college? He said, "Don't hustle me, son, the future is not yet in view."

I had known Jamie in hundreds of situations, at hundreds of parties, on hundreds of afternoons, when he was raised up and when he was beaten down, when he was drunk and when he was hung over, when the sun was shining and when his mood was black. But this was more than a bad mood. The light in him, that great mischievous glimmer, had gone out. I wondered what happened out west. What was he not telling me? I thought of my favorite movies (*Lawrence of Arabia, Sullivan's Travels*), and how in each of those films the action is structured around a pivotal scene, an event that forever alters the hero, that fills him with meaning or sets him on the path to glory or on the road to ruin. But in this film, Jamie's film, the pivotal scene had taken place off-camera, on the other side of the country. So here I was, left to re-create that moment from a few scraps of circumstantial evidence: the slump of his shoulders, the drag of his voice, his end-of-the-world sadness, and how everything in him seemed dead. "What about Las Vegas?" I asked. "How did my napkin trick work?"

He said, "Oh, yeah, fine. " Then he stubbed out his cigarette, sighed, and said, "Let's get out of here."

Jamie had lost his interest in the variety of life. He would sit for hours on his porch staring at his toes. He spoke under his breath, or in clipped sentences without meaning, or blandly of great events. The color had gone out of his face. His eyes were as cold as embers. Even in the same room, he was far away. He said nothing about his trip. Everyone was worried about him. It was an epic of sadness, and it overwhelmed our little world. We decided, in the last week of the summer, since my parents were out of town, to throw a marathon party for Jamie, which we hoped would lift him from his funk. I filled the refrigerator with food and sangria and made up the beds in the guest bedrooms and set out pictures I had taken in happier times: one showed me and Jamie with linked arms at Wrigley Field, another showed us in a toy store battling with croquet mallets.

Late in the afternoon Ronnie drove me to Evanston, where we bought beer from an Indian who, because we were young and stupid and knew just a little of the history of the world, we called Gandhi. On the way, talking about the real Gandhi, Ronnie said, "Some people are nice and some people are good, but Gandhi, now that was a great guy!" Then Ronnie grew very somber. "Maybe there is something seriously wrong with Jamie," he said. "Maybe it is something that even a marathon party cannot fix."

I said, "Ronnie, there is nothing that a marathon party cannot fix."

When we got home, the street was lined with cars and my house was filled with people. Some were girls from school, some were friends from the beach, but most were people we had never seen. It was a windy end-of-summer night, and I could smell pine needles burning. I found Jamie in the backyard laughing and drinking a beer. Tom put the speakers in the windows so we could listen to R.E.M. and the blues. Ronnie came out of the house with a glass of Old Grandad. He had never tasted alcohol before. Ever since he began lifting weights, which he had done in hopes of escaping abuse, he refused cocktails, saying, "My body is my temple." Again in hopes of escaping abuse, he now wanted a drink. He was soon going to college and so planned to advance into that club of whiskey drinkers he was certain existed out there in the world. He threw back his head and swallowed. He wiped his mouth and said, "OK if I have one of those beers?"

Within just a few minutes, I could see the liquor take its effect. Ronnie slouched into his own shoulders and his movements turned loose and easy. Then something truly strange happened; it is something I have never read about, or seen on television, or anything. Ronnie Flowers, who had never been east of Fort Wayne, Indiana, began to speak with a British accent. A Yorkshire accent, really, slang from the factory towns of northern England. He slapped Jamie on the back and said, "Eight boys, eight for nine and they as shy as heifers. You'll never fill a bag, but the ones you land you'll be glad you landed." We were mystified. At last, Jamie surmised that, late one night, Ronnie must have fallen asleep before a television set that was airing an old John Ford movie. "It must have gone straight down into his subconscious," said Jamie. "Besides, that is how Ronnie has always wanted to live. Just another one of the blokes yammering away in the pub."

I had intended to look after Jamie, to care for him, to nurture him, but I got drunk and started to have fun and then really worried about no one but myself.

Now and then, Ronnie shotgunned a beer or threw back three fingers of whiskey, shouting, "Aye, mate, ain't we friends after all!" Tom did back flips to impress the girls. If ever he learned the truth—that these flips impressed the boys far more than they ever did the girls— he would have been horrified. Tyler White was in the bathroom, adding and dividing floor tiles. Rink Anderson kissed a girl like someone in a Norman Rockwell painting—leaning forward, hands behind his back, lips outstretched. I was with Jamie in the attic listening to music as the party raged below. In the manner of Roman senators, we occasionally entertained a visitor from the lower floors. "Tell me," Jamie would ask, "are the people happy?" The party waxed and waned, ebbed and flowed; in the mornings, my friends slept in guest beds or on floors. In the afternoons, when I took a shower, I set a vodka and orange juice on the sink, which I sipped as I shaved. I felt like Bobby Darin.

On the third night of the party, Jamie and I drove to the town dump, to throw out several Hefty Bags of empty beer cans. As I parked alongside the Dumpster, a cop pulled in behind me, party lights flashing. A moment later, he was at the window. I could see only his uniform and the brim of his hat. In an ominous cop voice, he said, "What are you boys doing out here?"

I said, "We have come to throw away some trash."

The cop said, "Where is this so-called trash?"

I said, "In the hatchback, sir."

The cop said, "Can I see this so-called trash?"

I said, "Be my guest."

A moment later, I heard the cop poking through our empties. He said, "Oh-ho-ho, *that* kind of trash!" I looked at Jamie. He was laughing. Then the cop was back in the window, saying, "Who bought you this trash?"

I said, "We made it ourselves, sir."

"Look at it from my point of view," said the cop. "I got underage kids driving around with a load of trash they are not authorized to have."

He took out a note pad and wrote down our names. "I am not letting you discharge this trash at this site," he said. "Furthermore, if I find this trash in any public Dumpster at any time over the next two weeks—and I will be looking, boys, believe that—then I am coming after you with all of my power. Take this trash home and show it to your parents."

Jamie and I drove to the Sheraton Hotel by the highway and dumped the bags in the parking lot.

As the week dragged on, friends began to drift away. The party was a train making stops in the country, and at each stop a few people got off. It was strange. One minute, a friend would be just as ragged and poorly drawn as me, and the next minute he was as fresh as a new painting, hair still wet from the shower, chinos and button-down shirt, holding a suitcase. He walks from room to room, shaking hands, saying his good-byes. "Well, it's been an honor to know you!" And he is off to college: North Dakota, or Indiana, or Minnesota, or Iowa. Tyler White was gone, and then Rink Anderson, and then Jordie McQuaid, and then Ronnie Flowers, saying, "Good day to you, chaps. Good day!" One afternoon, as I was sitting in the yard, Tom Pistone came out in pleated pants and a cloth coat, a bag slung over his shoulder. He said, "So long, boys, I'm off to Normal." And then it was just me and Jamie, laughing and drinking, spinning through the night. And then Jamie was shaking me awake and I was looking up at him as if I were on an operating table hazy with anesthetic and he was showered and neatly dressed, saying, "Hey, little brother, I'm off. Gonna catch a ride and see if I can enroll in that big school they got out there in Kansas. I stashed the last six-pack in the wall. William Burroughs lives in Lawrence, so it can't be all bad."

I fell back asleep. When I woke up, the sun was low in the sky. I walked though the empty house. The rooms had been scrubbed clean. Jamie is a neat freak. He often said, "Destroy what you must but clean what you can." I stood in the driveway. After a while, my parents came home. We had a farewell dinner. That night, I lay awake in bed listening to the wind and to the message it was carving out of the dead air. It was speaking of farewells and voyages, how roads lead on to roads. In the morning, I showered, put on clean clothes, and left for college.

Part Two

In the fall of 1986, I arrived in New Orleans. I had left a gray, sober, Germanic city and all at once found myself in a drunken, weedy greenhouse of a town. New Orleans looks like a capital in the French Antilles, a port backed by swamps. Tulane is in the English quarter of the city, and the houses are ramshackle and Victorian. The leaves cast spiky shadows, and the vines running up the carports glisten in the drenching tropical rain. Each afternoon, I would climb up to the roof of my dorm, where I could look out over the neat greens of campus to the twisting coil of the river, tugboats heading toward the Gulf of Mexico. In the evening, the sun dropped through bands of dust and the sky passed through the colors of a mood ring—placid, agitated, angry.

I fell in with a group of boys from the dorms, prep

schoolers from the South with names like Whit and Ricky and Trey, who wore white bucks and backwards baseball caps, who loved Hank Williams Jr. even more than Hank Williams Sr., and who greeted you from a distance, shouting, "All right, son, let's go drink a couple!" After class, we would wander past the rundown mansions of the Garden District, with open doors offering a quick glimpse of marble and velvet. We talked about music or sports or high school, and I told stories about Jamie, which, late at night, grew into legends. On Saturdays, we walked down flat streets to the levee, the Mississippi River catching and reflecting the midday sun, so muddy the water looked like chocolate, and on the other side the smokestacks and industry of Algiers. We sat on the grass and imagined each other's hometowns, but I knew these friendships were just a temporary alliance. Whenever I found the chance, I slipped away.

Jamie was still very much at the center of my thoughts. I knew he had gone to Kansas, or so he had said, but I could not really imagine his life there. He did not write in those first weeks, and his mother, when I called, had also not heard from him. Once, in a bar, I met a girl who was visiting from the University of Kansas and, when I asked if she had heard of Jamie Drew, she said, "Drew-licious?" So somehow the nickname had tagged along. Well, that was good news, anyway. He was staking out his legend. Also, I knew some other kids that went to KU and from them there were rumors that Jamie had moved on to serious drugs, or was drunk all the time, or was seen with the worst kind of people in the worst kind of dives. And then there was still that other life that he lived in my mind. I thought of him whenever things went badly for me, when a girl shut me down, say, because in such moments Jamie gave me that special loser's solace: "Oh, baby, you've made a terrible mistake. You should meet my friend Jamie; he and I are superstars back on the shore." Just the memory of Jamie could make me feel that way. And of course I thought of him on those great nights that just went clicking along. At times, I felt like a fisherman, netting colorful experiences that I would enjoy not now so much as later, back at home, in some dark bar, where I would share them with my best friend.

A few nights a week, I would ride down to the French Quarter. The streetcar ran past brick walls painted over with advertisements, my favorite being the sign for HERMAN AND SON PAINTERS, benevolent old white-haired Herman over the words TWENTY YEARS' EXPERIENCE, next to his son, dark-eyed and mischievous, over the words FULLY INSURED. I would ride to the end of the line and then walk into the narrow, twisting streets of the French Quarter. The French came here first, settling at the end of the seventeenth century, building a haven for Jesuits and businessmen fifty miles from the mouth of the Mississippi River. Then came the Spanish, then the French again, then the Americans. The city has always been the great drain of the continent. It stinks with the sadness of the last century. From open doors you hear foot-stomping and horn-blowing. Is there anything better than standing in the street and listening to horns? Or going around the corner to Felix's Oyster Bar for turtle soup, or having a drink at the Napoleon House with its open shutters and its ceiling fans? Like Venice, New Orleans is a monument that has been allowed to dilapidate, an aristocrat pulled from her horse and gawked at by men with money belts.

Of course, some people feel that if a pleasure or a place such as Royal Street has been discovered by yokels, by happy idiots, by guys on convention, then it is ruined and must be abandoned. Or, worse yet, it is ruined and so can be enjoyed only through a heavy filter of irony, a cheese-cloth thrown up between yourself and the world. To me, this response is cowardly, an excuse to abandon the field to the yokels. It is running in the face of fire. So while other kids at Tulane avoided the Quarter, I spent many nights there, drawn to the same world that Jamie and I once looked for in the blues. From each trip I brought back some image or impression—a parrot-colored house glistening in the rain, a sloop plowing through the coffee-colored river—that I could turn over in my mind.

But most of the time I was just another kid on campus, far from home, lonely. There was a sense of abandon at Tulane that struck me as slightly insane. It seemed that many of these kids had come here on a spree, hoping at last to test the lessons of their parents or simply to flush them away. Of the twenty or so people on my freshman floor, only about five were around to graduate. The rest transferred or dropped out or burned away like debris on reentry. In Spanish class, I sat next to a kid who, on his desk, in addition to his notebook and pencils, set down a fruity cocktail—bright blue in a curvy souvenir glass, with straws, umbrellas, and a slice of pineapple. The teacher, a bug-eyed Honduran, spotted the drink and said in Spanish—everything in Spanish—"And what is that?"

"A Blue Hawaii."

The teacher ordered the kid to throw out the drink. The kid said that, since he was eighteen, his drink was legal, and since it was a Blue Hawaii it was refreshing, adding, "And, of course, it is delicious."

The teacher told the kid he would have to make a choice, so the kid gathered his notebooks and pencils and left with the cocktail.

Another day, I came to the same class after sharing a joint in the dorms. I was late and the chairs had been arranged in a circle, and this was confusing. As I sat down, the teacher said something to me in Spanish. It sounded like gibberish. I said, "Come again?"

He said *"Tengo"* or *"Tenga"* or "Tony," and there was something about *"la luz."* I somehow got the idea that I was being asked to turn off the lights. I reached over and flipped the switch. The room was in the basement, so all at once we were plunged into darkness. I could hear the other kids laughing. The teacher said something in angry gibberish.

I said, *"¿Cualo?"*

He said, "Richard, turn on the damn lights."

By November, I had at last found my way into a group
of friends, most of whom lived in a house a few blocks
from campus. The house had crooked shutters and a sag-
ging porch and was set before a curtain of swaying pine. If
you stopped by the house, you might find rooms alive
with conversation, or a party about to spill over, or just
kids sleeping it off. The boys in the house were pitied and
envied by the other kids on campus, because they were
idle and lawless and wild. They dressed in torn jeans
or dirty shorts, in shirts with no buttons and torn cuffs. In
the winter, some wore chewed-up black overcoats that
dragged along the ground. They went to class only if
moved to do so and slept where they fell, on couches or in
yards; now and then, when they tired of the city, they
headed north to the forests of Mississippi, emerging a few
days later with stories and game, and shared both in big
cookouts behind the house.

I would stand in the backyard, talking to each of the
boys, trying to find a way into the world they had built.
There was Joseph Rivers, a gloomy, dark-eyed Texan,
who wandered far from the familiar haunts, seeking out
desolate places. When Joseph fell into a black mood, he
would walk to a fraternity bar and pick a fight with a guy
twice his size, and the beating he took always made him

feel much better. There was Kip Clawdell, whom everyone called Crawdad, a creature of the great indoors, of
skunky rooms, gossip, late-night talks. There was Tim
Tree, so tall and sallow he looked like he had stepped
from a painting by Velázquez. Tree spoke of binges and
bar fights. Fog seemed to roll from the pauses between his
sentences. There was Magna Para, short and stocky, with a
glass eye. Now and then, Magna Para dropped his eye into
a beer, chugged the beer, and caught the eye between his
teeth. He called himself Cyclops. There was "Handsome"
Hansen Jackson, the only son of a local judge, who, each
February, so they could play at his Mardi Gras party, fur-
loughed a combo of jazz musicians. Hansen was clever
enough never to say anything anyone could understand.
He spoke of the inanity of college professors, the porten-
tousness of Hegel, the insipidness of rock lyrics. I did not
like him at all. There was Maximilian Franco, a sophomore who failed out the semester before. In the middle of
the year, Franco's father hired two goons to kidnap Franco
and return him to his home in Paraguay. In addition to a
blue blanket and a student ID, Franco left behind a Nin-
tendo, which, over the next three years, traveled from
room to room, driving down grades and ruining friendships. It was called the curse of Maximilian Franco. One
afternoon, Joseph Rivers, a liberator whose name should
be remembered with that of Simón Bolívar, hurled the
game off the second-floor balcony, smashing it to pieces
and freeing the house.

For the most part, these kids had met in the dorms, or at parties, or out at the bars, and they had been drawn together by a shared sense of style. This was not necessarily something they themselves possessed or even understood; it was instead something they badly wanted to *be*. Some of them called it *keek,* as in "He has keek," or "Very keek," or "Feel the keekness." If you asked them to explain *keek,* they would say, "Explain *jazz*." I suppose *keek* was a way of carrying yourself, of looking at life: of never being wrong-footed or buried by a situation or suckered by fake writing, or fake music, or fake anything. It was being in the right place at the right time, or creating the right place simply by being there; it was enjoying whatever moment you were living without judging it for its value. Did they drink, did they take drugs? Yes, yes of course, but not with that tired old hippie idea of enlightenment. They took drugs because there were drugs to be taken and because drugs were fun to take. In keek, I recognized a quality I had first seen in Jamie, whom I came to think of as the complete possessor of keek, a natural aristocrat who, whether he knows it or not, is down here slumming with the rabble.

The creators of keek, those who brought the ideal of it to Tulane, anyway, were three guys from Missouri: Waxey James, Eli Tenafly, and Matt Congress, called Congolese, or Congo. Congress would often say, "If you can talk you can sing, if you can walk you can dance—a saying from the Congo." These friends had known each other as kids, and they had with each other a total ease. Each of them had been a successful high school athlete, and there was something gone to seed in even their smallest gestures. Eli Tenafly had dropped out of school years before and was simply hanging around, drawling in an accent of no known territory. He was crafty and could read weakness. Once, when my friend Billy had, for the first time, taken a tab of acid and was wavering between here and there, he met Eli Tenafly, who said, "Billy, I want you to know something: you are never coming down." Waxey James wore leather pants and snakeskin boots with steel tips. Though he was not yet twenty-two, his hair had gone completely white. Once, driving by late at night, I saw him skulking around the Desire Projects. And Congo? Well, Congo was going crazy; anyone could see that.

It was Congo who brought me to the house in the first place. We met in a bar, drinking side by side, talking about the beauties of back home. From the start, he spotted me as another kid lonely for the Middle West. He had the face of old America—sharp cheekbones, wide eyes. We would meet at the house, then go out to the clubs. At one point, he told me he was drinking too much and so had decided to cut back to three cocktails per night, which sounded like a good idea until he told me the cocktails—a pitcher of beer, a sixty-four-ounce daiquiri, a double bourbon. After a fight with Eli Tenafly, he moved into his own apartment. He often lost his keys. Rather than hire a locksmith, he would sleep for weeks on the couches of friends. Someone bought him a key chain with a beeper: clap three times and it beeps. Once, after I had not seen Congo for several weeks, he came into my dorm room, clapped three times *(beep-beep-beep),* collected his keys, and went home. He wore one set of clothes until they wore out. He used to stand in the back of bars, face to the wall, drinking alone, saying, "Why, yes; yes of course."

In the early evenings, we went to Miss Mae's Place, a dive by the river where the drinks were cheap. From there we went on to Frankie & Johnny's for oyster or shrimp po-boys and pitchers of beer. And then to one of the music clubs uptown—Tyler's or the Maple Leaf or Tipitina's. Up front at Tipitina's there was a cast-iron bust of Professor Longhair, and we used to joke that, miraculously, the 'fro on the Longhair sculpture seemed to be growing. We often went to Jimmy's, a converted warehouse in a sketchy part of town. Dozens of local bands played at Jimmy's, the Uptown All Stars and Charmaine Neville, and good out-of-town bands, too, like Drivin' N Cryin' and the Pogues, but my favorite band was Dash Rip Rock, three young guys from Baton Rouge whose shows were always furious and wild. Their music was a combination of country and punk, what the band called cowpunk, with an occasional ballad for the girls. You always felt, at a Dash Rip Rock show, that you had stumbled onto the real thing. Now and then, the band played a parody of an old hit, including "(What the Fuck Is?) La Bamba," and a lightning-fast version of Jim Croce's "Time in a Bottle." Their own songs were always about something I had actually experienced ("All Liquored Up") or hoped to experience ("Shake That Girl"). I once saw the lead singer, Bill Davis, perform an entire set in nothing but an Indian headdress; this was during Mardi Gras.

Between sets, we wandered outside into streets lined with shanties, creaky iron dwellings blue with the light of flashing televisions. Underground bars were run out of some of these shanties, a slab of wood polished to a high shine, serving Thunderbird and King Cobra, a knockout malt liquor. Inside were black dudes in pimp-colored clothes. I never got up the courage to go in for a drink. Instead we went around the corner to Carrollton Station, a cavernous hall that twice a week staged a chicken drop.

You crowd into the bar with the country boys and the rednecks and the college professors and the sociology students and the girls from Loyola as the juke box blasts Merle Haggard ("Two Lane Highway"), or David Allan Coe ("You Don't Have to Call Me Darlin', Darlin' "), or George Jones ("White Lightning"), or Willie Nelson ("Blue Eyes Crying in the Rain"), or Johnny Cash ("A Boy Named Sue"), or Hank Williams Jr. ("A Country Boy Can Survive"), and wait.

The floor of the bar has been divided with tape into one hundred squares, each numbered. For a dollar, you buy a square; you can buy as many as you want. When every square has been sold, the crowd starts to chant. The cigarette smoke is so thick the faces in the crowd dull into a smear of color. At last, a chicken is set down in the middle of the floor; you watch as, to cheers and boos, the chicken bops its way across this arena of drunken faces. The chicken hesitates, scampers, clucks, pecks, feints, scratches. And at last the chicken defecates. If the chicken defecates on your square, the square you hold deed to, you walk away with the pot—one hundred bucks, a fortune. You always feel a little bad for the chicken, of course, and you never do win, except when you win, and at such times you feel only admiration for the chicken as you set off on a night of pleasure, every man your friend, every woman too. But usually you are back at Jimmy's for the second set.

Much later we would go to Bennie's, an after-hours club in one of those clapboard shacks built for poor families before the Second World War. From a distance, the bar looked like a music box, alone on its dark street, bursting with noise. In a comic strip, it would be surrounded by jagged lines. On the outside, it was no different from the other houses near Magazine Street, but it had been gutted and there was a stage in what had been the kitchen. The crowd squeezed in, no more than twenty or thirty people at a time. There was no cover charge and the music did not get going before 3 a.m., but on that makeshift stage you might see the greatest musicians in the world. They came from gigs at the big arenas; their shows had ended and still they wanted to play. During the Jazz Fest, when musicians came to New Orleans from all across the country, you might see a local guitar hero playing with Michael Stipe, or Marcia Ball backed by Stevie Ray Vaughn, or who knows. Between songs, an empty water bottle was passed around. Patrons stuffed in dollar bills, quarters, watches, rings. When we left Bennie's, we were always surprised to discover that the sun had risen and people were on their way to work.

At some point each night, we would stop by the house where the boys lived and try to scare up some action. If there was a bit of foolishness I did not want to engage in, Congo would say, "Son, these are just adventures. Now, wouldn't you agree that a young man needs his adventures?"

We often sat around talking to Eli Tenafly, who lived in a room in the corner of the house, in which everything, even the stains, were stained with some other kind of liquor, backwash, or fluid. Tenafly would sit there, rubbing his forehead, smiling. He was keek as hell, of course, and full of great stories, and not wrecked by ambition. He was just getting stoned until his money ran out. And, as I said, he was low-down and cunning and absolutely able to read fear. The ceiling of his room was strung with a web of Mardi Gras beads. This was the playing court for a game he had invented called Jake the Snake. Sitting on one of the room's low couches, you would throw a rubber snake up onto the net of beads; if the snake landed safely on top of the net, you got to give out a drink, or a hit, or a line of cocaine, or whatever you were playing for. There were dozens of rules, which you could learn only by breaking; each broken rule incurred a penalty drink or whatever. Some of the rules included Roughing the Jake (knocking loose a strand of beads), Banking the Jake (rebounding the snake off the wall), premature eJakeulation (throwing the snake before someone has finished their drink, line, hit, whatever). The Jake Court was strung with Christmas lights, and when it was dark the lights were shut off for a game of Night Jake. Some questioned the purity of Night Jake, which, they argued, lacked tradition.

For the most part, however, Tenafly preferred to play straight pool: that is, to sit alone in his room and get stoned or drunk, or else he liked to sit with just one other person whose mind he could manipulate. Perhaps because I am an open book, he took an instant liking to me and was forever asking me to hang out in his room. One night, I gave in and agreed to match him hit for hit, drink for drink, line for line. Even Congo was surprised. "Why would you want to do that?"

"Adventures," I said.

"That's not adventures," said Congo. "That's stupid."

I sat in that room smoking with Tenafly for hours, as again and again he loaded his pipe. At one point I began to shiver, and I could feel the curve of my spine and the fluids moving in and out of my organs and I knew for certain that I was going to die, so I looked up at Tenafly, who was breaking up marijuana on a tray, and he felt my eyes and he looked at me and smiled and said, "No, sir, we still gonna get a lot higher than this!"

When I closed my eyes, it was like being carried away in a swift river. Me on my back, swept by the current, looking at trees and cliffs and a faraway sky. I was certain I would never make it out of that room, out of the maze of rooms and streets that had become my life. Even now, years later, in my bed in New York, I sometimes wonder if I ever did make it out or if I am still in one of those rooms, head back, eyes glassy, dreaming.

In those weeks, it felt as if I were actually growing younger. Day by day, I was shedding that premature little-brother wisdom that had once—to some degree, anyway—kept me on the straight and narrow and so protected me and cheated me from that simple, pointless foolishness that is, after all, at the very core of keek. I guess I was never older than I had been at age thirteen.

In the morning, however, it was like the tide had washed out, leaving nothing but debris and headache and dry mouth and regret. OK, maybe not regret, but at least that sense of surprise that goes by the phrase, "How did I do that?" In this mood, I felt empty and sick for the Midwest, for the change of seasons, the sound of fallen leaves, the smell of coming snow, friends and family. I called my parents. As my father spoke, I could hear his office chair creak and the scene quickly arranged itself in my head: Herbie, in a bathrobe and beetle boots—the only shoes wide enough for his too-wide feet—at his desk on the second floor, looking out at the yard, the leaves turning red with the autumn. "Keep your options open," he might say. "If you work hard, you can still get the hell out of there and transfer to a decent school."

And, yes, I called Jamie but just about never got him, and I wrote him dozens of letters, filling him in on each detail, each development of my life. If he wrote back, it was a homemade postcard, a picture of himself: on a dusty street, in the window of an abandoned house, in a yellow field. I studied the foreground and background of each shot, imagining the life my friend lived just before and just after the shutter snap, how he bundled up on the first cold days of winter.

Our relationship had changed, of course; it was now less coherent and more episodic, following the inevitable course of childhood friendships when those friends have left home. No longer an unbroken current, the drama now played as a series of scenes, jump cuts. Jamie would come, Jamie would go, and the seasons would spin off into years.

Four or five months went by, and there was a knock on my door. I was lying in bed, looking out the window at the strange hazy tropical sky that settles over New Orleans. I crossed the room and opened the door. A voice said, "Hey, little brother, think you can let me in?" It was Jamie. He was wearing a wool coat for that cold Kansas wind, and his face was chapped and raw. He looked like he had crossed from the other side of the world. I was surprised to see him, so I hung back. I have always been shy on first meeting people, even friends. Jamie knew I meant nothing by it. He just smiled at me. I caught my reflection in his pupils—a convex little man, hands thrust deep in his pockets. Jamie said, "I came here to see you and to see the Mardi Gras, so c'mon, man, show me around."

He dropped his bag on the empty bed—with the use of some old-school shenanigans, I had been able to score myself my own room, the much-dreamed of single—and we set off across campus. It was like crossing the deck of a great ship, heaving with the waves, nodding to the other members of the crew. I was proud just to be out walking with Jamie, showing everyone I had such an interesting high school friend. It was like coming from good stock. People stared at Jamie—his loping stride, how he socked himself and said, "So here I am!" Or, "Little brother, we got some things to do!" Or, "Look at these trees, man, do you realize you go to school in the land of palm trees?"

To come down here, Jamie had ditched a week of classes at the University of Kansas, but he said it was OK because it was "field research." I asked how he made the trip. He said he had caught a ride from a friend of a friend as far as Jackson, Mississippi, and hitchhiked from there. When I asked his opinion of Lawrence, Kansas, where his school was, he shrugged and said, "It's a half-ass town full of forward-thinking types and a grocery list of alternative scenes. Its parents have declared a war on drugs."

We went to the house where the boys lived, and I took him from room to room. We found Congo at a desk near a window. It looked out on the backyard and the Dumpster. He was writing in his journal. As he stood to greet us, I stole a glance; the entire page was covered with the sentence, "Yes, yes of course." Congo shook Jamie's hand and then asked Jamie several random questions: "Have you ever made anyone cry?" "Do you follow anything that you call *policies?*" "What do you think of the term *pet peeve?*" "Have you ever sold anything to a friend?" "What is better, a roller coaster, a haunted house, or a water ride?"

Congo then turned to me and said, "I really like Jamie."

When you introduce an old friend to a new friend and they don't judge each other, or hate each other, but actually like each other—that is one of the greatest pleasures in the world. "Why don't you head over to Fat Harry's?" said Congo. "You can even take my car."

"What about you?"

"I'm gonna get back to the writing," he said.

Fat Harry's is a rundown dump, as dank and ominous as a bear's cave. Hours drift by, people come and go, but nothing really changes. Even on clear windswept mornings, it feels like the middle of the night. There is a bar in front and a grill in back. From the door you can see St. Charles Avenue shadowed by a lacy canopy of Spanish moss. Streetcars clatter past, washed-out faces in the windows. And then it is night at Fat's, regulars wandering in from odd jobs, the jukebox switching from Miles Davis to the Rolling Stones.

Jamie and I had a few beers and a few glasses of whiskey. Every third song on the jukebox was the "Mardi Gras Mambo"—"Down in New Orleans, where the blues were born, it takes a cool cat to blow a horn"—a scratchy trumpet-filled tune by the Hawketts, which is the true anthem of the New Orleans Mardi Gras, heralding the storm as surely as a covey of birds flapping across a thunderhead.

There was a strange moment of silence. Then everyone at the bar ran into the street. People lined St. Charles Avenue for miles, some seated in rickety bleachers, most on foot. Soon we spotted the parade, the Crewe of Bacchus, another one of those restricted old-white-boy clubs putting on its show for the drunken peasants of the city. First came the majorettes, batons playing tricks in the air, then the swaggering horn players in starchy white uniforms, marching hats and chin straps, and white boots. Black boys from all-black high schools razzmatazzing it down the street, shuffling side to side, swinging trumpets and trombones. Each marching band had the name of its school on its uniform: De la Salle, Brother Martin, Cabrini. One was called Cohen. Jamie convinced a majorette to give him a shirt—COHEN stitched in red lettering across the chest.

The street vibrated with footsteps; the horns shuddered through my limbs. It was spectacular. Then came the grotesque, vulgar, billowy, Day-Glo floats and the members of the Crewe in white clanlike hoods and masks, and the women as fluttery as French queens in petticoats, tossing out plastic beads, which the crowd fought over and prized. Behind the floats came the torch carriers, shabbily dressed black men on foot, shuffling under a shower of coins, grimacing in the orange gaslight, a haunting throw-back to the days of Reconstruction. "It presents a dilemma," said Jamie. "If you throw a nickel, you are a bastard. And if you don't?" Then came the last marching band, a caboose of a kid in back, sleepy-eyed, maybe failed two grades, raising his cymbals: *crash!* The sound swept over the crowd. Mardi Gras had begun.

We did not see my room for many days. We slept on couches, or on floors, or in backyards. We were often in the French Quarter, in the street or in hotel lobbies, a drink in hand, blue or red, juleps or Hurricanes. Rounding a cor-ner, we would stumble upon noisy crowds, girls hanging from balconies. There was no sense of cause-and-effect to any of this, no logic. It was a train wreck of images—a run-on sentence, a puzzle pieced together wrong.

At one point, we stood in a biker bar downtown called the Dungeon, laughing and slurring and holding each other up. Some old guy bought us a drink. He was alone and full of talk. "You boys are damn young," he said, "so I just hope your generation is better than mine. My genera-tion has done nothing. We did not survive a depression or win a war, we did not lose a war or go on pilgrimage, we did not immigrate or emigrate. Our lives have been just a collection of aimless conversations in smoky bars." He thought for a moment, then said, "Just like this one."

We hitched back up to Jimmy's, where Dash Rip Rock was playing. It was night. It was always night. The night went on and on. Mardi Gras is a night that lasts six days. When morning comes, it is not morning but just another version of night. Jamie said, "Let's take drugs."

I said I could get us a joint.

Jamie said, "No, real drugs."

We went to the house, where we found Tenafly getting stoned. He took us into his room. We smoked. Touching Jamie, he said, "Feel the keek coming off this kid." I found a book Tenafly had stashed behind his bed. It was filled with pictures. I read a story written in a fairy-tale type. A voice actually seemed to be reading the words into my ear:

In a land on the other side of the Black Sea lived a powerful King. One day, a peasant visited the court of the King, who gave the peasant a duck and said, "Kill this duck where no one sees." Many years later the King found the peasant, who was still holding the duck. The King said, "I told you to kill the duck where no one sees." The peasant said, "Yes, but the duck sees."

For some reason, maybe because I had been up for days, or because I had been drinking and drinking, or because I was just feeling the effects of the joint, the kicker of the story sent me into a swoon. In my head, over and over, I heard that voice say, "Yes, but the duck sees. Yes, but the duck sees. Yes, but the duck sees." For a moment, I felt I would never do anything with my life; there would be no escapes, and no guilt-free moments, and no end to my wandering, because wherever I went I would find the duck, and the duck sees. As I teetered on the edge of the abyss, Jamie yanked the book from my hands, tossed it across the floor, and said, "Don't read that shit. That shit will make you crazy."

Tenafly had let his sideburns grow, which gave him the look of a lost, road-weary trucker. He was laughing as he looked through an old-fashioned doctor's bag. He said, "Don't worry. In here is the cure to whatever ails ya." He handed two pills to Jamie, who said thank you and dropped the pills into his breast pocket.

It was a relief to get outside. The sun was coming up, and there was a gulf breeze, and the streets were damp and mysterious. Jamie said, "You are free and clear, little brother. There is no duck." It was a twenty-minute walk to the levee. When we got there, we sat on the grass and looked at the river. My mind cast into the future. I saw myself as an old man, writing reminiscences of my youth.

Jamie said, "Where are you right now?"

I said, "I am thinking about much later."

"You are not where I told you to be," he said. "You are somewhere far down the road, which is nowhere, and here I was, looking for you in the five minutes from now. Drugs are the only way I can think of hauling you back into frame."

He handed me a pill.

"What is it?"

"Something better than Ecstasy."

In those days, Ecstasy was still in its first youth, and so it wandered the countryside, raising hell. We all knew of its origins, how it was engineered in a laboratory somewhere overseas where a forward-thinking chemist believed he had at last found the key to the pleasure center—to a fast, carefree place in your otherwise mournful, envious brain. We knew too that for several years the drug had been legal, off the charts of the police, and some spoke of those years as a lost paradise. I told Jamie that I was afraid of the drug, and besides I was already drunk and stoned.

He said, "You have hit a wall. Take the pill. Climb over."

Over the years, there has been a lot made of peer pressure, almost all of it bad. Peer pressure—kids telling other kids how to behave—is said to make people do stupid things, drink too much, run wild, vandalize, shoplift. Mothers, pointing out the logical fallacy of peer pressure, often mention the Brooklyn Bridge and how you shouldn't jump off it. But in my life, peers—and here I am talking mostly of Jamie—have pressured me into doing many things I would certainly not have done on my own, and in almost every case these have turned out to be the great adventures of my life.

Jamie said, "Take the pill."

I chased it down with warm beer.

As we walked to Magazine Street, Jamie told me his theory of life. It was based on the Winnebago. Here is what he said:

"Every kid knows about the Winnebago, right? It's a myth, a dream. I mean, every kid, given a choice, would choose a Winnebago. This is a house we are talking about, but it's on wheels! When you get tired, or bored, or life is just too much, then fuck it; just drive away. But as you get older, you forget about the Winnebago. Or maybe you are made to forget. You come to believe that the Winnebago is just the opposite of a good way to live. You come to see it as stupid, or low-class, or whatever. And so this knowledge you had from the very beginning, like so much of that first pure childhood knowledge, is drummed out of you, and soon they've got you lining up in the ranks of the apartment dwellers! So you see! You have been forged into forgetfulness and brought into society! But some of us, a remnant, a fucking holy remnant—we have never forgotten. We hold on to the dream of the Winnebago."

Somewhere along the way, as Jamie was talking, the drug kicked in. It was like one of those science-fiction movies, where, as the trusty ship shifts into warp speed, the stars—there are always about a million stars out there—turn from stationary points into streaky lines, and then—*wham!*—the ship is catapulted clear to the other side of creation! And that's just how I felt: like I was flying through space, with the stellar wind in my hair, and galaxies and quasars racing by, and far below—isn't it beautiful from this distance?—the twinkling settlements of man. I guess I was smiling a luckiest-man-in-town smile, because Jamie leaned over and looked into my eyes and said, "It kicked in! And it looks good! I'm right behind you, little brother, and I can't wait!"

And then we were both reeling down Calhoun Street, giggling and hugging, and the sun climbing higher. We turned onto St. Charles and made our way to Fat Harry's. It is strange to walk into a bar at seven in the morning and find it still reeling with its nighttime crowd: kids at the jukebox and the pool tables, bartenders pouring drinks and the girls sipping Coronas, Jason and the Scorchers on the stereo, and everyone laughing and waiting for the next parade.

Jamie and I found a place in the corner so we could lean. The morning drifted by in a dazzle; the music poured through me. Sometimes, as I looked at a girl, or out the door at the trees, or at the efforts of the bartender, I would forget that Jamie was even in town and then, moments later, discovering him at my side, I would smile and shout, "Oh, Jamie! Hey! It's you! Wow, it's great to see you!" His pupils were so dilated that his eyes were no color but black, each eye a camera, the lens wide to capture this strange scene. He had his jaw thrust out and he was grinding his teeth. I was doing the same. Looking around, I saw that everyone in Fat's was doing the same: this face, the telephoto eyes and outthrust jaw, was a shared mask. Everyone was on Ecstasy. Everything was booming.

As we listened to the music and talked to girls and raced into the street, where it was morning, and back into the bar, where it was night, I realized that this was turning out to be one of the great days of my life. I felt like I was using up something that had collected inside me over many years; that a pair of hands had lifted my brain from my skull and was squeezing out the juice in one mad rush. And the result was a euphoric, charming me, empathetic as hell. At the bar I talked to Jon Close, a kid I had long considered a fool, a big dumb guy, with a gaggle of drones in his wake.

Jamie said, "I thought you hated that guy."

I said, "Yeah, I do. But you know what? He's got a point of view!"

Sometimes Jamie wandered off, and when he got back it seemed he had been gone for years, had crossed mountains and oceans, had lived lifetimes. We greeted each other like long-lost friends. At one point, he said, "You have more in common with everyone living today, even with those poor emaciated bastards you see starving in

Time magazine, than you do with anyone dead, even your own grandfather or, in my case, my own father, who died tragically young. And it is not just that you have more in common with them in comparison to a dead person; you really have everything in common with them, just by the simple math and great miracle of being alive; and you and me, who grew up in the same town, we are brothers and that is not even our choice. It is no more a choice than it is your choice to have Steven as your real brother, who, as you know, can be moody as hell, except of course, I am your real brother just as much as he is—more, because I fulfill my fucking duties."

We decided that we should make a movie of this day as seen through our eyes and call it *Two Dudes at Mardi Gras.*

We decided we should go downtown to Zulu, one of the great parades of Mardi Gras. Congo's car was still parked behind Fat Harry's. I told Jamie he should drive.

Jamie said, "Do you realize how fucked up I am?"

I said, "So is everyone."

He said, "Yeah, well, here is something I never told you. My father died in a drunk-driving wreck. He just had a couple of beers, but it was enough to send him across two lanes of traffic into a speeding truck. They had to pry him out of the wreckage."

Jamie had tears in his eyes. I started to cry too, and I hugged my friend. I told him I was sorry, to forget it, we would find some other way. After a long moment, he said,

"You know what just happened? Two dudes at Mardi Gras just became two responsible dudes at Mardi Gras."

We congratulated each other and went outside to hitch. The bar had emptied out and there were no cars. We stood out there forever.

Jamie said, "Fuck it, I'll drive."

As he got behind the wheel, he said, "Two responsible dudes at Mardi Gras just realized Mardi Gras is no place to be two responsible dudes at Mardi Gras."

He buckled his seat belt, checked the mirrors, and started the engine. As we pulled out, a car stopped directly in front of us. It was a cab. It was empty. Jamie said, "See what just happened here? Two dudes at Mardi Gras just had responsibility thrust upon them."

The taxi sped us along Magazine Street, the shops twinkling like cheap jewelry. I stuck my head out the window and lapped at the wind like a collie. The cab turned sharply, and for a moment my face seemed to hang over the street like an effect in a Saturday morning cartoon—my eyes bugged out, smoke came from my ears, and then my head snapped back.

Jamie said, "Easy, boy."

We got dropped off on Canal Street, where the few tall buildings of the city gather in conference. At Mardi Gras, the towers look as uncomfortable as men on the beach in business suits. Some of the buildings were covered in mirror glass, and you could see the sky reflected, the clouds as sluggish as wet cotton. I stood under a tree that must have been two hundred years old; the limbs were twisted like rope. I was amazed at the beautifully effortless way it climbed into the sky. The leaves shifted on the breeze, and with each gust they filled up like sails. The leaves were so green and so soft they looked like fur. I said to myself, "Whatever else happens to me, I will always have this tree."

"Here it comes," said Jamie.

In the distance, I could see the tall floats of Zulu. We fought our way to the front of the crowd. The men and women on the floats were dressed like storybook versions of old Africans, in war paint and elaborate headpieces, earrings, and nose bones. They shouted and danced and moaned. The parade began years ago as a put-on, the black community's response to the all-white Crewes of Mardi Gras. In addition to beads, the marchers tossed out spears with rubber tips and coconuts. Every year, a few dozen people were brained by a coconut. In the economy of Mardi Gras, where beads can be traded for goods and services, mostly sexual, there is nothing more valuable than a spear from Zulu.

Midway through the parade, Jamie grabbed a spear. It was like watching him take a bolt of lightning from a stormy sky. The crowd cheered. Across the street, a beautiful girl motioned to him. He said, "I am just going over to see what it is about, and I will be right back." I told him not to go. "It's too hard to cross. You will never find your way back. We have to stay together." But there was so much chaos and noise, I don't even think he heard me. He just said, "I will be right back."

Two feet from the curb, it was as if he were swallowed under the surface of a great river. A cop yelled at him. He vanished and a moment later surfaced on the other side of the street. I saw him talking to the girl, and he turned around and turned around again and then was lost. The sun glittered off the trumpets. The drums pounded. His spear disappeared in the crowd. For the next few days I encountered him only in stories, the battlefield reports of friends, or the friends of friends, who had seen Jamie on the street, in a bar, at a parade. He was moving through the city like a dervish, a step ahead of the crowd, of the cops.

In New Orleans, during Mardi Gras, a black bus with black windows ghosts through the streets. If a cop sees something he doesn't like—maybe it's a fight, or someone pissing on a curb, or someone smoking a joint, or maybe it is nothing at all—he calls for the black bus, which is never beyond the next corner. And so here it comes, bounding through the evening smoke, with a tangle of stunned girlfriends and angry mothers in its wake. And out of the bus come a half dozen officers in riot gear, each face a smear behind its plastic shield, and billy clubs waving. And, just like that, it is over, another sucker loaded on the black bus. When the bus is full, it drives to Central Lockup, the city jail, where holding tanks overflow with the thousands of players who have lost at the game of Mardi Gras. If, after two days, no one comes to claim a prisoner, he is moved to Tent City, a fenced-in field on the outskirts, an echo of the Great Depression, a Hooverville of prisoners sharing cigarettes and telling hard luck stories. "Aw, man, this motherfucker got me coming out of Fat's with a fistful of pills."

Many times that week, with the hours drifting by and no mention of Jamie, I feared he had been taken away by the black bus. But always, just before I went to bail him out, some bright-faced girl would race up and say, "I just saw your friend Jamie. He was over on Rampart Place. He was marching behind a band and shouting *Payday!*" Or "Jamie is over on Freret Street, up on a float, dancing a shimmy." Or "Jamie bought a round of drinks at Frankie and Johnny's and vanished before the bill came. Even the bartender got a kick out of him." When discussing Jamie, people spoke in three tenses: he was so fucked up, he is so fucked up, he is going to get so fucked up. Each time I raced off in search of my friend—to Rampart, to Freret, to Frankie and Johnny's, where I paid the bill—he had always left just a few minutes before. "No, man, he's gone. And too bad. He's wild." At one point, I actually caught sight of Jamie in the distance, on a wrought-iron balcony on the third floor of one of those old French houses on a back street in the Quarter. His eyes were closed, his arms were moving, and the sun cast shadows on his face. I shouted and waved but he didn't hear me. There was a bouncer at the door, and though I pleaded he would not let me in. And then Jamie was gone, on with his batlike flittings across the city.

On Fat Tuesday, I was in the French Quarter, standing amid the strip joints and tacky bars, squeezed by the clown-car crush of the crowd. The street was a tunnel of balconies twisting out of sight. The sky was filled with garbage and ash, and pieces of ash settled on my hands and stained my face. And then, exactly when it seemed there would be no end to this day, it got very quiet—the kind of quiet only a crowd can make. And before I knew it the crowd was being pushed, jostled, driven down the street. Up ahead, I could see a blue wall of cops. Within a few minutes, we had been forced into the drab, empty blocks of the business district. I was suddenly aware of the sun. We had been pushed from nighttime back into the day. In the distance, the police stood around talking. Behind them, municipal employees went to work with hoses and trash cans and brooms. Mardi Gras was over.

I took the streetcar to Napoleon Avenue and walked through the Garden District: boulevards deserted, houses dark, cars snug in their carports. Here and there, a shop owner was sweeping a sidewalk; cabs ghosted by. Otherwise the city was asleep, drifting through its collective dream, each breeze carrying soft snores and *zzzzz's* rising like smoke from the chimneys. In the dorm, many of the doors were open and I could see the boys tucked into their beds, still wearing souvenir caps and beads. When I opened my door, I saw Jamie in my bed, stripped to the waist. The blinds were down, the slats filled with light. I touched his shoulder. He sat up, rubbed his eyes, and told me, as best he could remember, what he had been doing over the last several hours. And then he hesitated, and stammered, and shut up. It was as if he had suddenly realized that his stories, no matter how well told, would not keep, that their essence would not survive in the everyday world. So instead—and he would do this more and more as he got older—he just stopped talking. I suppose he had decided instead to keep his adventures in his mind, where they would lose none of their strangeness.

I lay down on the other bed and was asleep before I untied my shoes. It was 4 p.m. I slept through the afternoon and the night and did not wake up until the next morning. I could hear voices in the street, and trucks and cars, and I knew that the strange city of the Mardi Gras was already gone. My shoes and clothes had been taken off and were stacked neatly on a chair. I found a note on the desk:

> Gotta get back. See you in Chi.
> ——Jamie.

After finals, I packed my bags, went to the airport, and caught a flight home. From the window of the plane,

Chicago, that great smoky town, rose out of the tablelands as clean and colorful as rock candy. Ronnie met me at the airport. He was driving a low rider with tinted windows and Little Feat on the tape deck.

In just one year of college, Ronnie had executed a complete identity change. He went from clean-cut would-be jock and proud member of the hundred-pound club—Ronnie, at two hundred pounds, could safely bench-press three hundred pounds—to groovy drugged-out stoner, aviator glasses to hide his bloodshot eyes. He had begun the year at the University of Iowa, where he was a dashing frat boy; had gone, after a semester of failing grades, to Carl Sandburg College in Galesburg, Illinois, where he was a lost youth; and ended the year at the University of Miami, where he bought a gun, smoked his first joint, and killed targets at a shooting range. As we merged onto the tollway, he said, "If you want to score some dope, I got a man in Kingston. And don't worry 'bout customs. He packs the shit in coffee beans."

In those weeks, I did not know what to do with myself. In many ways, I felt I had left this town behind and was now a man of the world. On occasion, I even called a movie a film or referred to a famous writer by a nickname. "So anyway, I was out in the woods, but of course I took old Doc Percy along." And yet here I was, back in Glencoe, no place better to be. So I just wandered around, amazed at how tame and lifeless and sleepy and bland and

empty and small everything seemed to me. Each afternoon, Tom Pistone came by in his GTO. He wore
T-shirts and jeans, sat with boots on the lawn, pulled at
the grass. Tom had cut his hair short and, as in the story
from the Bible, had lost some part of his strength. Once
the toughest kid in school, he had now become just
another guy on the sidewalk. His friends still treated him
with the greatest respect, though, as you will continue to
call a president "Mr. President" even after he has been
voted out of office.

Jamie had taken a job painting houses. It was his own
business, set up with some of the local boys. Kansas was
cheap but not free, and Jamie needed the money for rent
and tuition. For him, it was truly a summer of hard work. I
would see him only at the end of a long day, wiped out
but trying, with that deep, rough workingman's tan, his
boots dusty and speckled with primer, and his chest
swelling from his trips up and down the ladder. He said he
dug the view from the scaffolds: the geometry of low
houses, porches and shrubs, front yard, pool in back, a girl
sunbathing.

If it rained, he would show up at my house in the early
afternoon. If my father happened to be home, they would
crash side by side in the family room, watching my
father's favorite movie, *Gunga Din*. By the second or third
scene—Cary Grant fighting off a band of howling fanat-
ics, killing for the love of Kali—they were both dead

asleep to the classic summertime sound of rifle shots and tribal whoops coming from a beat-up TV. Otherwise, if Jamie got off late, we went down the street to get high with Ronnie and to watch him eat. Jamie said Ronnie had become a stoner because dope heightened his most acute passion—food. When Ronnie was stoned, his eating habits were indiscriminate. He ate jelly beans with ketchup, bananas in pickle juice, dry packs of instant oatmeal. One night, I opened a tub of butter in his refrigerator and saw where he had scooped a hunk, his finger marks as well preserved as prehistoric vertebrae in amber—the remnants of a lost civilization. "No more aesthetic concerns," said Jamie. "Ronnie is now down to the guts of the matter."

I suppose this is the place in the story where I should say something about my father and how we began to fight, calling each other names, and how these fights turned violent because he did not understand me and would not let me grow up, because he was old and I was young. Maybe, for drama, I should say that Jamie, who had no father, moved in to fill the void, becoming closer than I was to my own dad. After all, I spent my first conscious years in the 1970s, when the notion of the generation gap, of sons against fathers, of a necessary patricide, became a social religion. Our after-school specials were full of it, as were our Movies of the Week. But the truth is, there never was anything like that between my father and me. Maybe each of us just believed too strongly in the comedy of everyday life, or maybe we just liked each other too much, or maybe, more realistic and less bothered than my older siblings, I was just not shocked to discover that my parents did not know everything. Don't forget: I grew up after all those wars and hearings and scandals. I knew the world had fallen. If the world has fallen, everyone in the world has fallen too. Even my father. (But still I had *Caddyshack* and Bill Murray to say "Gunga, ga-lunga, gunga.") So instead, in a very natural way, I began to drift beyond the old man's jurisdiction.

My mother was angry at me that summer—for doing nothing, for coming and going, for "using the house like a hotel." At last, for my own protection, I began to look for a job. And that is when my real summer began, what I call the Summer of Bad Jobs. I spent most of June walking in and out of offices, cinder-block buildings, mall restaurants. I was questioned, looked over, filed, and rejected. At the end of the month, I was offered a job at Danny's, a day camp for rich kids out in what my friends and I used to call Comanche Territory, the prairies in southwest McHenry County, where once, at a festival called the Taste of McHenry, I sampled fifteen different kinds of custard. Danny, a pot-bellied, buck-toothed rah-rah-rah suburban dad who often said, "We are about the *we* and not the *I* here at Danny's," fired me just three days into my second week, for, according to him, forming, among the seven-year-olds, a "cult of personality." In his office, he spooked me by saying, "You are not the same Rich Cohen we hired."

Who is this other Rich Cohen, I wondered, and will we ever meet?

A few days later, I was, in essence, picked up from waivers, hired on by Poppa George of Poppa George's Pizzeria. The first night I was put in charge of something called the Beef Bar, where we served spaghetti cooked in what Poppa George called the "North Shore style"—a fistful of noodles held under a lukewarm tap. This was, said Poppa George, "our little secret." At the end of my first shift, Poppa George, who was a foul-tempered old man, ran a finger across a plate I had not rinsed properly and said, "Boy, I'm disappointed in you."

I said, "You've known me for less than five hours, Poppa George. If you are disappointed in me, you're a fool."

Poppa George slapped me and I quit.

Then, in the strangest twist of the summer, I was hired, irresponsibly, as a counselor for mentally and physically handicapped adults. (My first New York résumés still carried this job, a ghost of some forgotten existence, listing my duties as "Supervising field trips, driving the handicapped van, dispensing medication.") My charges were schizophrenics and other crazies. When I got home, my father would say, "Let's hear it," meaning the many surreal things that happened to me every day on that job. An old female mental patient told me she had found a penis in the trash, "a darling little penis." At the bowling alley, a schizo, lip-smacking from a megadose of L-dopa, heaved a ball down the carpet into a Coke machine. A young woman who had no disability other than sheer meanness greeted me by saying, "Good morning, motherfucker. And I bet that's what you do: fuck your mother." On my birthday, she gave me a card that said, *You're my favorite counselor, you little bastard.* There was a tremendously fat patient named Wilbur who told me I looked like a young Jose Ferrer. Another patient, given the wrong pill (by me, by accident), recited a haiku and then passed out. One rainy day, for kicks, I brought Jamie along—the mean lady called him a shithead and Wilbur said he looked like Prince Charming, not in the film but in the illustrated books.

By the beginning of August, having burned out, I was working on a road crew and as a part-time janitor for the Winnetka park district. It was as much responsibility as I could handle. We built playgrounds and cleared dead trees, and after storms we shoveled roadkill into the back of the park district truck. Most of the other members of the crew were drunk drivers sentenced to community service. Our bosses were the same lifetime custodians whose secret world of mop closets and playground cigarette breaks I used to wonder about in grade school. So now here I was, one of the boys, exchanging banter and shirking duties, taking the landscaping truck out on personal business. I spent most of my time with Santiago, a hardworking immigrant who wore overalls and floppy hats and had the dark, handsome face of a figure on a Mexican mural. Sometimes, a few of the convicts and I went off to get stoned—we hid in a scaled-down student-built replica of Abe Lincoln's log cabin—but Santiago always found us. Creeping past the butter churn, he would shout, "You must produce!"

At the end of the summer, Santiago and I stripped and waxed the floors of the Hubbard Woods school. I crossed the room with the mop, spreading solvent. Santiago hummed by with the stripper. When I told him I wanted to run the stripper, he said, "You will lose control, smash up the room, and burn a hole in your foot, and your rich parents will sue poor Santiago."

After much hectoring, Santiago let me run the stripper. Before he had even turned his back, I lost control. The stripper buzzed across the room, knocking everything to pieces. It was headed for my foot when the engine died. Sliding through the solvent, Santiago had yanked out the plug. He said, "You see! I told you. Now you must produce in the old way—with the mop."

Most of the time, I was in the basement with a half dozen janitors who had worked at the school for years, arriving each day, summer or winter, before dawn. One of these men was born in Romania and had fled through the mountains when the Communists came to power. When we screwed around, he said, in a heavy accent, "You dammed kids think you got the world by the ass!" His beloved son, who was my age and worked at the school, was always running off with the truck to get stoned on the beach. The rest of the janitors were just working-class guys. There was a father-son team. The father was in his nineties, waiflike and frail but still smoking a half pack of Marlboros before breakfast. He would sit there grumbling in his ribbed T-shirt, a butt dangling from his thin lips. Too old for anything else, his job had narrowed to just one task: he painted doors. Not walls, not fences, not trim, just doors. There was a tennis day camp behind the school and one of the counselors was a beautiful girl who wore short little skirts and was always flipping her hair. I thought of asking her for a date but chickened out, fearing the social divide (janitor, teacher) was simply too great. One day, this girl went into the ladies' room in the school to change her shirt, and it just so happened the old janitor was in there painting a door. He came back to the basement, saying, "I seen it all, every bit of it, her little boobies too."

By the end of each day, I was as worn out as any other working man in America. Sometimes I would stop at a lonely spot along the shore, cut down the bluffs, strip off my clothes, and jump into the lake. I would then drive to Sloppy Ed's. It was a sad time at the hamburger stand. A few months before, in a divorce settlement, Ed had lost control of the business. His wife, Rachel Carter, had taken over—a slight strung-out woman, in over her head but making a go of it. Ed, who by court order was not allowed inside the stand, stood on the sidewalk, shouting, "You can serve hamburgers! You can put on the mustard and the pickle and even the secret sauce. But you will never be Sloppy Ed."

Ed became a biblical figure in our town, singing out his sorrow. At night, he holed up in a road motel, his hair wild, his cheeks as red as ground beef. I asked if he wanted me to stop going to the stand. He said, "No, I want all the worshipers in the temple. That way, when the false priest is driven from the altar, the services can resume without delay."

Most of the time, Rachel Carter just ignored Sloppy Ed. Now and then, however, she wiped her hands on her apron, stepped into the street, and said, "Why, tell me, why would I want to be Sloppy Ed? I divorced Sloppy Ed!"

This would humble the old man. He would start pacing. "OK, fine, you don't want to be me!" he would shout. "You don't love me! OK. You want to divorce me. Fine! But why steal my birthright?"

Of course, this is just the sort of scandal Jamie and I would have spent hours discussing. "It's a split in the very center of town," Jamie might say. "It is a call to choose up sides, progress or tradition, legal documents or human soul, boys or girls, shirts or skins."

But Jamie was not around. He painted houses from early morning into the sundown. And even when he was around, I did not have time for him. By then, I was giving every moment—that is, every moment not concerned with stripping and waxing floors—to a girl who had climbed quickly through the ranks from stranger to crush to girlfriend. Jamie let it be known that he did not approve of this new girlfriend and that in losing myself to her I was in some way violating his teachings.

I met Sandy at a party in Winnetka, introduced by Haley Seewall, who said, "This is the prettiest girl in Lake Forest." If Haley had not said that, who knows what would have happened? I have always been highly suggestible. In the future, whenever I looked at Sandy, I heard Haley saying, "This is the prettiest girl in Lake Forest." She had long blond hair thrown to one side, and her eyes were big and brown and she was wearing a blue shirt. She always wore blue. Maybe blue was her favorite color, or maybe she just knew she looked good in it. She said, "I am so drunk I am spinning."

Only later did I learn the entire story of that night. Sandy and I spoke over the keg; Sandy went outside and kissed some other guy; Sandy came back inside and talked to me some more; Sandy went back outside and threw up in the bushes; Sandy went to the bathroom and swallowed mouthwash; Sandy went home with me. The night ended with me following a confusing traffic of mumbled signals: Go, Stop, Yes, No, Yes, Stop, Crossing, Yield, No, Yes, Go.

Sandy soon made her first daytime visit to my house. Stepping into the kitchen, she said, "I almost ran over your yard man." A few minutes later, my father, covered in peat moss and fertilizer, came in the back door and said, "I was almost run over by a girl in a fancy car." Of course, Sandy did not know that my father was a fanatical gardener; that he worked in the yard for days at a time; that he was often seen by the neighbors gardening at night; that he had been forbidden, by my mother, from gardening for more than three hours at a stretch; that, so he could evade this edict, he purchased several sets of identical clothing; that when my mother left for the grocery store or the pharmacy, he would race out for a few stolen moments in the garden; that, on my mother's return, he would quickly race into the house and change from a dirty striped shirt and muddy khaki pants into a clean striped shirt and clean khaki pants; that, on one such occasion, he was given away only by his white shoes, which had turned black. Needless to say, my father took an instant dislike to Sandy. He said, "Just being around a girl like that, you sustain a loss in brain tissue."

On weekend mornings, Sandy would drive to my house, sneak past my parents, and climb into my bed. She was a former Miss Teen Great Lakes. No kidding. There was a full-length picture of her in the window of the Glencoe Photo Shop. In it, she was smiling with her hands on her hips, her teeth glossy, and her hair all brushed down one side of her head. It was a kind of symbol in our town, that photo, in that it seemed to stand for something else, though I could never figure out exactly what. It was very uncool, that's for sure; still, in those weeks, I found myself carrying a copy of it around in my wallet.

This was no ordinary girl. Her mother had divorced and remarried, and her stepfather was a practically illiterate multimillionaire, jug-eared and sour and constantly complaining, throwing money at his stepdaughters— three girls standing before him, shouting, "Gimme! Gimme! Gimme!" And him: "Take it! Take it! Take it!" Sandy said she hated him. At fifteen she had run away, stuffing some cosmetics into a bag and calling for a limousine. She charged the getaway car to her stepfather's account, which made it easy for him to track her down; she was at a friend's house in Kenilworth, watching cartoons and getting high. She spent two nights in a guest bedroom and then went home, again by limo.

We were together every night, eating picnic dinners and drinking warm beer. I will never forget how she looked coming out of the lake. Even the silly times leave distinct memories. At that age you are essentially longing in the shape of a body. One afternoon, I borrowed the park district truck for a made-up errand and drove to Lake Forest. It was raining. The streets unwound before me, swinging into focus: the trees, the houses, the glistening yards. When I turned onto the main street, there was Sandy in a yellow slicker, hair stuck down to her face. We went to my house; the yellow slicker was tossed into a corner. Each day, she gave me a gift—hair gel, money clip, cologne—until, piece by piece, she had turned me into a different person. At night, we went to Ravinia, a bandshell in Highland Park, to see the Chicago symphony or modern dance. Or else to a high-falutin' suburban restaurant where they treat you like a sophisticate. Her father said, "If you go to Froggies at your age, what can you possibly look forward to later in life?" But Sandy had it all figured out. We would be married after I graduated from college, and a few years later she would be pregnant, and then we would have three kids and I would be riding to and from the city on the commuter train. One night, as we came out of the Village Smithy, the swankiest restaurant in Glencoe, we stumbled into Jamie. He was walking home from work. He gave me a look that said, You poor bastard.

When my parents were out of town, Sandy lived in my bedroom. We dragged the television upstairs, so we could have sex and still watch David Letterman. What I remember best is not the way her body felt—this I remember not at all—but the way her body made my body feel. One night, I drifted off and awoke many hours later, with the TV showing an ape running full tilt up a rocky slope. When the ape cleared a ridge into a valley, where hundreds of apes, each wearing a leather leisure suit, were gathered, he raised a hairy fist and shouted, "Brothers, the humans are attacking! One ape is injured and another is dead!"

At the time, our housekeeper, Dolmi, a middle-aged woman from Ecuador whom my mother considered a member of the family, was bothered by what was going on between me and Sandy and yet could see no way to stop it. So at last she took a pack of condoms from my room and placed them in my parents' night table. When my mom found the condoms, she was far too embarrassed to say anything to me directly. Instead, she called my sister and engaged in one of those endless late-night conversations that have had such a nefarious effect on my life, leading to big-sisterly talks on drunk driving, bounced checks, and AIDS.

On those nights when my friends came around, looking for a party, Sandy and I would shut off the lights and pretend no one was home. Once I watched Jamie drive up, park his car, and ring the doorbell. After a while, he stepped into the driveway and looked up at the attic window. I moved back, trying to fade into the darkness, like the tiger in the old print. But I know he saw me; it registered on his face. He shook his head, got in his car, and drove away.

Tom Pistone invited Sandy and me over for a party. He lived in a creaky house by the train tracks, a garage in back and a weedy yard. We were met at the door by Tom's father, who, for a father, was so young and so handsome that I always felt he was playing a trick on me. He was wearing a white T-shirt, his body just a cord of muscle. He said, "Get in here, boy! Come to see Tommy? Well, all right. Let's get a look at the girl. She ain't too bad!" As he said this, he walked around Sandy, saying, "No, sir, ain't too bad at all."

Tom was drinking a beer on the back porch, staring at the houses across the alley. At dusk, the lights in those houses came on, one after another, like the break of a wave. Then it was night. Jamie walked in from the yard in faded jeans. He asked if I wanted a drink. He went to the kitchen and came back with something that tasted like a hangover. Tom talked to Sandy. Jamie took my arm and said, "I need to talk to you alone."

"Not now," I said.

I did not want to be alone with Jamie or listen to the lecture I knew was coming. That night, I avoided rooms where he could back me into a corner. After dinner, I went into the garage, where Tom had stashed some beer. As I opened the fridge, light spilled across the concrete floor and I spotted Tom's father in one of the cars. It scared me to death. He rolled down the window and smoke billowed out. He handed me a joint and I took a drag. It was skunk weed picked on the far shores of Lake Michigan. "The hippies used to grow it," he told me. "It's the only true thing they left behind." He coughed a little, then said, "Nice girl you got there."

"Thank you, Mr. Pistone."

"I noticed her the moment you came in," he said. "She has nice hair and a good ass, and good tits too."

I told him I had to get back to the house.

"Now you're thinking smart," he said. "You don't want to leave a girl like that alone. Not for a minute."

I grabbed the beer and headed toward the house, glad to get out of there. I had always figured that, as you got older, you grew out of your boyhood weirdness. To me, Mr. Pistone was a warning that youthful creepiness can just as easily dig in and become your personality. From the porch, I could see the kitchen through the window. Light gleamed off the stoves and countertops. Sandy stood before an open cabinet, reaching for a glass. The shelf was high and she was on her toes. Her skirt rode up, showing her legs. Coming up from behind, Jamie put his hand on her back and reached for the glass. As he did this, he said a few words in her ear, and she turned and smiled. I did not think Jamie would sleep with Sandy. That would have been too simple for him, too simple and too drastic. After all, it was not Sandy he was concerned with, it was me: my friendship, my gaze. No. He was just showing me that for him having Sandy would be no more than a good night's work. After all, he had been with dozens of girls like Sandy, or so he let me believe. So no matter where I turned up, Jamie had been there first, been and gone. It was this aura of mastery, of keekness, that, among other things, had attracted me to him in the first place. It was the light he was giving off. But that summer it began to irritate me. It was an example I could not live up to. As long as Jamie was in my life, nothing I had would be truly my own.

And then it was the Fourth of July, which has always been my favorite holiday. In the afternoon, Sandy and I walked into town. There was a warm breeze and a marble sky. The houses looked festive, and the trees were draped in bunting. Some of the stores had set up sidewalk tables. The Korean guy who owned Ray's Sport Shop was doing a brisk business in whiffle-ball bats. Sloppy Ed was at Harry's Delicatessen, eating corned beef and saying, "I have lost my last appeal. I am cut adrift, no way home." The streets were flooded with faces, the faces that make up a small American town: women in sundresses with bronzed legs, men in hats, straw hats and Panama hats, fathers loping toward middle age, mothers cold in judgment, toddlers and kids dressed up for American Legion baseball, old-timers with hard gray eyes. I went into Little Red Hen and ordered the lunch special, a slice of pizza and a Coke for a buck. The pizza was greasy and delicious.

The parade began at the firehouse and stretched through the afternoon strange as a beach dream. There were kids on tricycles, bigger kids on bicycles, the mayor in striped pants riding one of those old-fashioned contraptions with a giant wheel in front and a small wheel in back; there was a high school jazz band and a junior high school marching band, and the kid on the snare drum got a nose bleed; there was every fire truck and police car in town; there were dozens of other vehicles, including the game warden in his panel truck flashing his lights, and a sleek police boat up on a trailer that got the crowd whispering. Chief Tompkins was a keen fisherman, and some wondered why he needed such a fancy rig if not for his own excursions. Bringing up the rear, on a sit-down lawn mower, was Tall Ted Conner, a retarded man in his forties who could be seen in any season racing his visions through the parks of town. Tall Ted weaved down the road, waving and smiling.

As the parade turned off the main drag, it seemed to take the afternoon with it. The crowd headed toward the beach. In less than an hour, everyone had regathered on blankets and lawn chairs on the bluffs above the lake. In Glencoe, it is the same fireworks show every year. The sun goes down; the crowd gets restless; there are shouts of anticipation. Then the first rocket goes up, trailing sparks. For the next twenty minutes or so, due to the small-town budget, rockets scream by in fits and starts, now and then a splash of color setting the town beneath a strange new streamer-filled sky. Otherwise, the night is dead moments, noisemakers, and duds. As a kid, I had watched these sparklers fade, hoping one would burn long enough to set the woods on fire. In the end, there is of course the finale: a run of consecutive blasts, the people ooohing and ahhhing.

Sandy said, "When will it start?"

And then the whole world went up, dozens of rockets sailing into the sky, bursts of light, sharp concussions echoing up and down the lakeshore. Everyone jumped to their feet. This was the best show ever. There were fiery candles and screamers and flashers. After that first flurry, however, the show settled back into its familiar pattern, with each burst separated by stretches of dead air. And then ten, twenty, thirty minutes went by with nothing at all. Not a burst, not a blast. Someone shouted, "What's going on?" Flashlights, dozens of flashlights, began wandering across the bluffs. Here and there, faces, dumbstruck and angry, were caught in the beams. It was the cops, walking through the blankets and chairs, saying, "All right, everyone, time to go home. Some idiot set off the finale first."

It was a play without a third act, an orgasm without sex, premature eJakeulation. The crowd turned surly. The sidewalks filled with grumbling celebrants. I ducked onto a side street and lost Sandy; she had been carried away in the crowd. Jamie was waiting on the next corner. In his baggy coat, he looked like one of the old men of town. "I was hoping to find you," he said.

I said, "Hey! What's up? What about that finale?"

He did not answer me right away. He paced back and forth, arms folded across his chest. His body language was all about confrontation. He was clearly thinking over what he wanted to tell me. I finally asked him.

"I want you to stop it," he said.

"Stop what?"

"You know, stop it," he said. "Stop all of it. Stop wearing cologne."

"What? What are you talking about? Why?"

"I want you to smell your own stink," he told me. "I want you to tear the pleats from your pants. I want you to stop playing house. I want you to rejoin the land of the living."

OK, I thought, so here it is. "You want me to break up with Sandy."

"Fine. If you want to reduce it to that, fine. I want you to break up with Sandy. Ditch her. Dump her. Get rid of her."

The back of my neck started to itch. It was hard to get any words out.

"What are you doing?" I said. "Are you jealous?"

He stopped pacing, thought for a moment, then said, "Am I jealous? Yeah, I guess I am jealous, but not for Sandy. I don't care about Sandy. There are Sandys enough for everyone."

"What's wrong with Sandy?"

"She is no good," said Jamie. "The girl is a drain. If you are sad, you can weep in your sorrow. If you are happy, you can get drunk on your beer. If you are with Sandy, you cannot be sad or happy. You can only be with Sandy."

.   .   .

I did not talk to Jamie for the rest of the summer. I heard stories about him from Tom and Ronnie, and I saw him at a distance, diving off Ming Lee or walking by himself in town. Of course I missed him and thought about him and wondered if he was thinking about me. I guess I was angry. It was not just about Sandy. Jamie and I had begun to drift apart while I was away at school, and that distance had only increased. Neither of us would ever live at home in quite the same way again. We were now visitors on vacation, just passing through. In those weeks, I realized—probably for the first time—that our friendship was tied to Glencoe and to the beach and that it would not necessarily survive forever. There might even come a time when it had faded, Jamie's name just another entry in my address book, a number dialed so infrequently it actually had to be looked up.

At the end of August, Sloppy Ed's burned down. I heard about it from Ronnie. He drove me uptown in his mom's car. When we got there, a crowd had gathered. Flames shot through the roof; firemen chopped through the walls; the burners popped like grenades; the steel sign, as symbolic to us as the Statue of Liberty, swayed and collapsed. It was the finale the town had been cheated of on the Fourth of July. The fire chief discovered evidence of arson, a crime that remains unsolved, a great mystery. For years, the stand remained as a ruin in the center of town. "I want to go to Sloppy Ed's," Jamie once said, "but the bastards blew it up!"

．　　　．　　　．

It was summer, it was winter, it was summer. Three years drifted by. Each fall, I drove to New Orleans. Each spring, I drove home. I made the trip with other Tulane students from the Midwest in sports cars or station wagons or, when I was an upper classman, in a car that, in hopes of giving me a life lesson, my father helped me negotiate for and buy in a used-car lot one afternoon in Lincolnshire. My first choice was a blue Honda Civic. Stenciled on the hood of that car was the name CHUCK. The driver-side door read BOBBY. The passenger-side door read BILLIE. Otherwise the car was in excellent shape.

I said, "It's perfect."

"Yes," said my father. "But did you see all that writing?"

"So what?" I said. "We'll paint over it."

"You're missing the point," he told me. "A schmuck owned this car."

We bought instead a gray, wheezy, salt-stained Dodge Daytona. In my mind I see it from above, wandering in and out of traffic, floating over the causeway across Lake Pontchartrain, which is drenched by green day storms that blow up from the Gulf of Mexico. In each flash of lightning, you see a sudden burst of landscape—weedy shores and rusty barges, trees straining in the wind. On these trips, I was usually with two or three friends, singing along with country music or listening to one of those overheated backwoods preachers on A.M. radio, laughing,

and then crying—crying for our sins and for the death
that awaits us all. The cities flew by like beacons: Mobile,
Jackson, Memphis. At night we listened to Top Forty,
shouting out the names of the songs, cursing the singers—
the great paradox of my age; too cool for our own
pleasures.

Or maybe we are heading south, getting into the car in
winter-bound Illinois, wearing layers of sweatshirts, the
defroster clearing a patch in the icy windshield. The outskirts are endless, factory yards and smokestacks reflected
in the oily water. Iron bridges span frozen streams. Gas
stations drift by. The broken lines waver. You can vanish
into one of these little towns, live someone else's life, the
years drifting by—it's the future, it's coming. Below
Cairo, the rivers churn to white water. There are leaves on
the trees. You stop for gas. The windshield is a cake of
dead bugs. You have crossed into a new season.

Senior year I lived a few blocks from campus in a house
of gables and overhangs with Kurt Zaminer and Seth
Coral, whom I had known since freshman year. Zaminer
was big and gentle, liked to be called the Crasher, was
often drunk, and managed a local bar called Clover. When
I went to Clover, the Crasher would pour me two shots of
whiskey, serve me dinner, and give me a handful of bills
from the cash register. Coral was short and dark, smart,
violent, and stoned, or else just about to get stoned, or

looped on some more potent drug. At the beginning of the
semester, on a visit to the State Fair, he traded a stack of
old Styx records for a pit bull that snapped at my ankles
and chewed on my fingers. If I was fresh from the shower,
the dog lapped the water off my legs, so that all year I
never once felt clean. Now and then, the dog disappeared
on what Coral called "a dog spree," running with the wild
packs, returning days later, scratched up, in the company
of a dozen strays.

The wall of my room was lined with French windows.
On moonless nights, I would throw open the doors, sit on
my bed, and look over the rooftops. I could see dark
clouds and wind-tossed trees and telephone lines, which,
running from house to house, seemed to stitch the city
together. During my time in college, there was never any
sense of the outside world, of newspaper headlines, or the
rise and fall of markets. At most, I knew that the Japanese,
once beaten, were now back at our throats. Otherwise, I
was in a room where nothing happened but tonight and
the night after that; these nights were, of course, adding
up to weeks and months, but this is something I did not
realize until it was too late.

Sometimes I drove by the house where the boys had
lived, the house of keekness. It was empty. The stories of
the house had been forgotten, the boys wiped out by
graduation. Like the ancient dynasties of Europe, each
had suffered his own collapse. There was Eli Tenafly, who
fell in the course of one long night, at the start of which

he banged on the doors of the closed public library—shouting "I want to read books!"—and at the end of which, taken away by the cops, he shouted, "Don't beat me up!" There was Waxey James, who one day was there and the next day was gone, or was seen in glimpses, wandering the streets along the Irish Channel. Congo called him "another poor weaver who has gotten hold of the wrong thread." There was Congo himself, whose fall was as glacially picturesque as that of the Ottomans. After quitting school, he passed through a series of odd jobs, in the end delivering pizzas, until one night, instead of completing a large order, he broke into the houses of eight friends and left a pizza on each kitchen table with a note, *A gift from the Congo.* I last saw him on the back patio of the Rendon Inn. He said he was leaving New Orleans and wanted to share one last drink, "something truly terrible." I ordered Mind Erasers. Congo drank his down and walked out. Years later, a friend told me that Congo was living with a migrant family in California, traveling with the harvest, picking grapes.

Of course, there were all those parties that thunder across senior year, when, facing the same uncertainty, you become friends with your enemies; parties that began at sundown and continued until the first flush of dawn. This was a time of exciting uncertainty, with kids going off to job interviews in distant cities, waiting rooms in glass towers. I was engaged in a struggle with my father, who wanted me to go to law school. It is his belief that a person with a law degree is a person protected from the ups and downs of life. As a kid, when I told him I wanted to play pro hockey, he had assigned me a favorite player, Ken Dryden of the Montreal Canadiens, because Ken Dryden, before entering the NHL, had first gone to law school and so he "always had something to fall back on."

I took the law school entrance exams but really wanted nothing to do with any of it. I want to be a writer, I told my father. We fought. And fought. In the end, he stopped talking about it. I congratulated myself. I had battled him to a standstill. I had become a man. I wrote up a résumé and sent it out to various national magazines. That spring, in addition to rejections from those various national magazines, I was surprised to receive rejections from schools I had never applied to, law schools my father had applied to in my name. It was like a girl that you have never asked out calling to say that under no circumstances will she date you. There were more than twenty rejection letters. My father said, "You want to be a writer? Good! I am teaching you about rejection."

That spring, Bob Dylan moved into a house not far from campus, a house surrounded by a fence that I imagined myself climbing. Bob Dylan would read my short stories and call me *the kid,* as in *Hey, how is the kid doing?* Each morning at 7 a.m., he ate breakfast at the Bluebird Café on Magazine Street. In a vague way, I planned to show up at the Bluebird, slide into his booth, and say something essential, which in the end I did not do because

I had nothing essential to say. Besides, I was busy with my own life, waiting for the future to unfold, drifting through the Garden District or heading out to the Jazz Festival, which is held in the swampy heat of the fairgrounds, a horse track approached down endless empty streets that unspool like loops of cartoon animation, miles of identical houses beneath a flat blue sky. Jazz Fest runs for two weekends in late April. I was out there every day, wandering the boozy crowds, the faces like flowers, swaying on the sticky wind. We believed, with graduation, our world was coming to an end. Coral said, "If you have any drugs, I suggest you take them while there is still time." We went from stage to stage, Dash Rip Rock to Clarence "Gatemouth" Brown to Beaujolais on his washboard. I ran into my math professor, a big long-haired Australian, who, not wanting to wait on line, traded me an A in his class for a six-pack of Budweiser. Walking behind a family on their way to the Arts and Crafts Center, I marveled at the distance between them and me. Sitting in the gospel tent, I watched as the St. Cloud choir, substantial flaxen-haired black women in pink and white gowns, tantalized me with thoughts of the afterlife, singing, "Heaven! Oh, yeah, Heaven is a place where I will lie around all day and watch TV!"

One afternoon I passed out at the fairgrounds and woke up in a car being driven by Coral, speeding in and out of traffic, saying "All right, all right, all right!" There was sunlight on everything, shining off bumpers, glancing off windows. We turned uptown and the sun was behind us and the stars came out and it was night. I passed out again. I woke up at a restaurant, a table of food in front of me. Mexican food. Crasher said, "Eat up, we've got a lot more distance to cross." And we wandered out into the narrow streets of the French Quarter, in and out of the lamplight.

We stepped into the Napoleon House; smoke hung above the bar. A crowd was gathered around a kid telling a story. People were laughing, buying him drinks. I could not see his face but there was the rise of his voice. The crowd burned off like fog and then the kid was alone—in blue jeans and a red cloth coat, face lean and handsome. I said, "Goddammit! That's Jamie!"

I felt like old Tom Sawyer spotting Huck Finn when, until just that moment, he thought he was dead. I walked around Jamie, touched him, asked a dozen questions. It was as if he had wandered into my dream. He said, "Your mom told me you were going for a job interview in New York, and since she doesn't like the idea of you making such a long drive alone, I volunteered to look after you."

When I asked why he had come to the French Quarter, he said, "I just got off the bus and walked into the first good bar."

I had not seen Jamie in months. His hair was tucked under his collar, his eyes were bright, his lips were chapped, and he looked thin and pure, as if he had shed every excess. For a long moment, he was a stranger to me;

but then, frame by frame, this new Jamie, this strung-out, whispery kid of the road, merged into the old Jamie—all the arguments and distance forgotten—until we were right back where we started, and time could not touch us.

It started to rain the morning of graduation, and by afternoon the streets were fast-flowing rivers and the radio broadcast news of the flash flood. The ceremony was held in an auditorium. Families gathered in the doorway, men in seersucker peering into the rain. My parents flew in from Chicago and my father carried my mother through the current. A man in a straw boater said, "The word for that is chivalry." That night, when Jamie and I got back to the house, Seth Coral was leaning out the living room window, shooting off bottle rockets, which exploded on the roof across the alley.

The waters had receded by morning, and the streets were strewn with debris. Seth Coral and the Crasher had already packed up and gone. So had everyone else. When it ends, it ends fast. Jamie and I walked through the empty campus. The trash cans were filled with notebook pages, some covered with equations, others with the inner meanings of great texts. Jamie read a page out loud: "Gatsby is you and me, and Gatsby is the American dream."

We packed my car and took a farewell drive through the city. The sun had come out and glittered off the storefronts and streets. The city, rundown houses and vines, more than ever looked like a port in the Caribbean. We stopped by Tipitina's on Tchoupitoulas Street, bought T-shirts, and listened to Oingo Boingo run through a sound check. We went to Domalici's, a legendary sandwich shop on Annunciation Street, and got oyster po-boys for the road. Then, for the hell of it, we swung by the Camellia Grill, a whistle-clean lunch counter on St. Charles Avenue, with black waiters in checkered pants, sandwiches naked or dressed, pecan pie, omelets.

We drove along the grassy levee, the overloaded Daytona grinding and bottoming out. The river stretched away to the gulf, its green banks under a blue tropical sky. We saw an abandoned ship in the last stages of dilapidation. It had been one of the great riverboats of polished decks and staterooms, but it was forgotten and rusty, with weeds on deck and vines in the pilothouse.

We reached the Huey Long Bridge at 7 p.m., with the sun dying in the flats. It carried us over the river and into a thicket of smokestacks. And then we were running in the dark, the city far behind.

We drove without saying a word, watching the road unwind, stopping at a Waffle House for pancakes. Jamie stood in the door, smoking a cigarette. We studied maps, followed whims, traveled hundreds of miles out of the way to tour a stupid stalactite cave. By moving we were at last standing still. One night, after not speaking for hours,

Jamie said, "You know, when I was a kid, I used to drive my mom crazy with questions. But my favorite questions were always about dying, and again and again I would ask her if I would ever die."

Jamie was driving. I had no idea where we were.

"So what did she tell you?"

"It bugged the shit out of me, but she always gave me the same answer," said Jamie. "She said, 'Yes, you will die but you will live forever in the hearts of those who love you.' And I smiled like this made perfect sense and like it was very good news but inside I was thinking, That really sucks! I mean, all those kids I ran around with will be at Great America riding the roller coasters and smashing the hell out of each other on the bumper cars, and maybe as they fly down a drop they will think about me, and that is how I live forever? I mean, I'm sorry, but that really sucks."

The Gulf Coast highway took us through Mobile and Pensacola. After a big lunch of oysters in Jacksonville, we followed I-95 into Georgia and then cut over to U.S. 17, a stop-and-go run of sun-baked beach towns. In Parkers Ferry, South Carolina, we sat in a honky-tonk listening to country music and eating grilled cheese sandwiches. In Honey Hill, Jamie got a haircut and stood on the sidewalk afterward, saying, "I'm the one should be having a job interview in New York. Just look at me!" On the way out of town, we passed a Lincoln Continental driven by a black man in a cream white suit, wife at his side, kids in back. "Why can't I be one of those kids?" said Jamie. "Or that daddy? Just for a day, why can't I live that life too?"

By the end of the week, we were blasting through the sweet blue pine forests of North Carolina. We checked into a motor lodge on the Atlantic Ocean, changed into our bathing suits, and stumbled across the highway to the sand. The beach was deserted. There was the strange sea-weedy smell of an incoming tide. Jamie went into the water. He swam out so far I could not see him. I stretched out and fell asleep. When I woke up, Jamie was at my side.

"How is it?" I asked.

"Incredible," he said. "I've never been in the ocean before."

For a moment, I just looked at the waves. Then I asked, "What about Reach the Beach? On that trip, didn't you swim in the Pacific?"

Jamie thought for a moment, then said, "Well, it didn't work out just the way I wanted it to."

"Tell me."

Jamie hugged himself; his eyes were as clear as lake water; he was on the verge of saying something. Then his mood shifted. His voice got high and tight. He said, "You see, on that trip there were all kinds of mix-ups that you absolutely have to plan for on the road and there were contingencies of course and backups that led only to more contingencies and more backups and so my adventures had to be found on the fly and in between the hassles but isn't that the way it always is?"

"So, what? You never made it to the ocean?"

"No."

Back in our room I closed the drapes and turned on the air conditioner. We could have been anywhere in the country. I got into bed and immediately vanished into that strange kind of dreamless hotel sleep that burns off everything that came before. I did not wake up until the middle of the next afternoon. My interview was in just two days. We took showers and got back on the road. Washington, Baltimore, Trenton. On every horizon were those vast brown buildings that signal the approach to cities. "I hate places like this," said Jamie. "Not the city and not the country, not even the suburbs, just nowhere." The closer we got to New York, the faster I drove.

We rolled through the Holland Tunnel into Manhattan—those endless, sweaty, car-tangled avenues. I stopped at Union Square. As I got my bags from the trunk, a cab was honking; otherwise we might have had a better good-bye. As it was, Jamie simply ran around to the driver's seat. He would take my car to Chicago and sell it. He got in, rolled down the window, and said, "If any of those big shots start riding you, just tell them you've got a friend Jamie who does not know or even care that any of them are alive." And just like that I was alone in the city, my bag over my shoulder, a list of phone numbers in my pocket.

Part Three

There were blue afternoons and muggy summer nights, a band playing in the back of a bar, air steaming up from the grates, sidewalks filled with sweet young girls, each the prettiest from her hometown—or else riding a subway down to the East Village, standing in the front car, watching the track unwind out of the dark, screeching into the station—those are my first memories of New York. I had taken a job as a messenger at *The New Yorker*. I had been offered more substantial jobs at lesser magazines but my father, who grew up under the spell of J. D. Salinger and E. B. White, said, "Better to Xerox your ass at *The New Yorker* than write a column for the *Daily News*." When I told him I intended to work at *Regardie's,* a magazine in Washington, D.C., he said, "How did I raise a schmuck for a son?"

The *New Yorker* offices were then on 44th Street between Fifth and Sixth avenues. In those halls it was still the old martini-fueled New York, writers sleeping it off on daybeds. I would deliver mail and packages around the city or lounge around in the messenger room, which was as forlorn as a train station out in the sticks. The messenger department was run by a wispy guy who protected his boys, most just out of college. We argued, competed, complained. Between errands, I ducked into the magazine's library, where I tried to give myself the education I had not gotten at college.

The most revered figure at the magazine was Joseph Mitchell, who, in the 1930s and 1940s, wrote his mystical stories about the lost characters of New York, legendary books of reporting on rats and shad fishermen and eel pots. Joe Mitchell published his last story in 1963, and his books had since gone out of print. You had to hunt for them in secondhand bookstores; there was a kind of underground traffic in his work. By the time I reached the magazine he had become a sainted figure, an elegant man with white hair, often in seersucker, who seemed to reflect a distant world. He came into the office each morning and worked at his typewriter all day and produced nothing. To ask after his writing was considered bad form, so I admired him from afar, his comings and goings, past and present. I knew he had grown up on a tobacco farm in North Carolina, that he began his career during the Depression as a reporter for one of the now defunct New

York dailies. I had been in search of the real world beyond the theme park which has taken the place, or so it seems to me, of every city and town in America. In Joseph Mitchell, I at last found proof of this other world—of the authenticity that Jamie too was after. His writing was modern and exotic, a guide to a city that had ceased to exist, a Constantinople lost under decades of advertising and noise.

One afternoon, though I had been told Joseph Mitchell was a recluse and the last thing he wanted was to be bothered by someone like me, I said, "To hell with it," and went to his office. I was nervous, of course—about the possibility of an icy reception and how the real man might shatter the image. But when I knocked, the door flew open and Mitchell leaned back in his chair and said, "Come in, come in," as if he had been waiting for me. He wore a rumpled suit, the sleeves rolled up, his eyes the same soft blue as the fabric. I explained my admiration for his writing, and he asked about my hometown and told me about his. He got excited as he talked and rubbed his palm along his bald head and stammered, as if the right words eluded him. When he could not explain just what he wanted to say, he showed me photographs of old New York, pier sheds and town houses. Pointing to a sign high on a brick wall, he said, "That is a ghost sign. It advertised a store that had already been gone for eighty years. To me such signs have always been strange and scary."

I told Joe Mitchell my biggest fear—that I had reached

the city too late and that the world itself had become a kind of counterfeit. "I felt just the same when I got to New York," he said. "I was too late. I said it to myself again and again: 'Too late. Too late. Too late.' And then one day, in these offices, way up on the wall, I noticed those same words, 'Too late.' And I began seeing those words every-where: 'Too late. Too late. Too late.' I found out it was James Thurber, from a world far older than mine, who had been writing them. So you see, even Thurber thought he had come to the city too late. And the people before Thurber? Well, they thought they had come too late too! That's the human condition. Wherever you go, you are by definition too late. You missed the whole show. Which, if you think about it, means that wherever you go, you can-not help but be right on time."

Before I came to New York, I thought I wanted to be a writer, though I was not sure what kind. A fiction writer, I supposed, because it seemed to me that fiction writers get to tell the best stories. The writing of Joseph Mitchell convinced me, however, that there is a shape to the real world and real life that is just as beautiful and strange as anything in the imagination. So I went from delivering packages to delivering packages *and* looking for places and people that I myself might write about: a suite in the Penta Hotel where New Jersey railroad workers, dozens and dozens of them, sleep away the afternoon in a single room; Eli Ganias, who, having caught a foul ball at a Mets game, found his life utterly changed; a mostly forgotten stone crypt in the middle of the city, traffic speeding all around, with the remains of a legendary Civil War general.

It was a great way to see the city, rambling block to block, searching for experiences that could be converted into stories. Or, as a good friend of mine said, "Into writing of some kind!" But really it was the city itself that interested me. Manhattan, squeezed between its two rivers, seamed with avenues and streets, as prickly and mysterious as one of those stalactite caves. I liked the fire escapes and how they looked against the brick walls, how exotic debris collected in the gutters, how Park Avenue wound through the Pan Am building, and Chinatown was another country at night, and the sun looked so good going down between the buildings. At night, I went to the Brigadoon Bar, so called because it appeared only rarely, when I was incredibly fucked up, out of the mists of the East Village. Stepping through the door, seeing again, as if they had never left, that same old cast of characters, I always felt a strange rush of assurance and said to myself, "So here I am again," meaning not just the bar but a peculiar mental state that fused this moment with the last such moment, though it might have been months before, obliterating all the moments between.

I found an apartment in Greenwich Village on one of those narrow streets I had imagined in high school, when

Jamie looked at my brother's photos and said, "New York, how can you beat that!" It was a fifth-floor walk-up on Grove Street with a skylight and a glancing view of Sheridan Square. In the winter, when it snowed, the tall buildings were hidden and the streets so quiet the city seemed to fall back into the nineteenth century. My friend Jim Albrecht hired a cabdriver to drag him (rope, skis) down the desolate storm-bound avenues. In spring, when the snow melted, the runoff seeped through the skylight and flooded my apartment. I got a bucket to catch the water. The super finally showed up. He looked at the ceiling and said, "I think you need a bigger bucket."

When I was not at work, or killing the day, I would sit at my computer, listening to Little Walter and writing about Glencoe. With my eyes closed, I could see the waters of the lake, the bonfires along the beach, the sidewalks freckled with leaf shadows. I wrote about Sloppy Ed's—the glory, the fall. I wrote about Jamie, road trips, double dates. On the page these memories became stories. In this way, they were preserved and destroyed, taken from my mind and fixed in place. Never again would they haunt me in quite the same way.

One of these stories was called "Always Be Closing." It was about Ronnie, who, after graduating from the University of Miami, moved to the Panhandle and took a job selling used cars. The idea of Ronnie Flowers, the most trusting kid I knew, assuming the totemic role of used car salesman was mind boggling. Ronnie described his job to me over the phone. He told me about his training and how he had studied from a manual called "Always Be Closing"; about spotting a mark the moment he or she steps through the door; about the high jinks of the financing shed; about Rodeo Days, during which Ronnie sold used cars (EVERYTHING MUST GO!) dressed as a cowboy, in a hat and chaps. My favorite stories were about the idol of the scene, the slickest stud on the lot, who had written a book of poems to chronicle his exploits:

> I track him like a fly ball, drifting
> back,
> and now I have him,
> fat with money, and
> hopes in the
> highway, so he leaves with a
> Le-
> Baron and
> without his
> cash,
> sucker!

Ronnie worked the job for two years. The week he quit, he came to see me in New York, sleeping on my couch and filling my life with statistics and lot talk. Each night, before we went out, he took a long shower, clouding the mirrors, his beauty products scattered across the shelves. He wore a thigh-length leather coat and a silver watch.

Now and then, he jiggled his wrist to adjust the watch. Or twisted his gold class ring. Or banged the ring on the table—*thunk, thunk, thunk.* He was screening a new image. After a few drinks, he would throw an arm across my back and say something he picked up at the dealership: "So where do you see yourself in three years? Do you have a five-year plan, or are you drifting?" In his voice, there was a corporate seriousness, an executive branch responsibility. Everything about him seemed to scream *I am in control!* In control of my once-runaway body; of my pores, which for years were filled with pus; of my image, which each afternoon, before the bell and after, had been dragged across the playgrounds of Glencoe.

I would stare at Ronnie, searching for the kid who, standing in the foyer of my house, believed my father when he said, "Ronnie, this is the Lord thy God." I could not find that kid anywhere, and it spooked me. I thought to myself, Where is my friend? Can a person vanish so cleanly into adult life? And: If this is not Ronnie, who is it? And: If this *is* Ronnie, who is Ronnie? In remaking the present, had Ronnie remade the past? Had Ronnie ever been Ronnie? And what about me? Have I also lost my childhood self? If so, where? When? Does that mean I am now an adult? And what about Tom Pistone? And what about Rink Anderson? And what about Tyler White? And what about Drew-licious?

Part Four

Jamie was at the University of Kansas for six years. Between semesters, to earn money for tuition, he painted houses or worked construction. When he graduated, his friends were gone. He packed a bag and went traveling. He passed through bus stations, small cities, and early morning landscapes. He returned to Glencoe in the fall of 1992. The trees were bare, the roads strewn with leaves. He moved in with his mother and grandmother. He went for walks—a soldier home from the wars. He had grown into a kind of hard elegance that never goes out of style; he was gifted. He recognized the joke even in sad stories. He was never fooled by hype. He carried a heightened sense of the real world. His presence alone changed a situation. In a sense, though no one was around to see it, he had fulfilled his promise. On Friday nights he got drunk downtown and went home with college girls. To them he was older, experienced, on the edge of a meaningful existence. He took a job with a road crew. In the evenings, he could be seen in town in work clothes. There were no cars on the streets; the stores were empty. His friends had gone off to law school, to girlfriends, to jobs in the city. He felt left behind, forgotten—a sketch of his former self, an outline, detail and color drained away.

Years went by. Young couples moved to town to raise young families. Old couples, having sent their children out into the world, moved away. My parents took their bow-out, my father making a final inspection of his garden, the vines and flower beds, the trees he had planted. As the house had yet to find a buyer, my parents asked Jamie to move in as caretaker. "You will at least get out of your mother's house and have a place to think," said my father. In the winter of 1995, with my parents settled in Washington, D.C., Jamie moved into my house, starting first in the attic and then making a steady progression from bed to bed until he unpacked in the master bedroom and started his new life, giving out the address and phone number that had once identified me as surely as my name or hair color.

It was as if Jamie was the last inhabitant of a lost city. He would wander from room to room, looking into drawers and closets. He stared at the clothes my father had left behind, signature garments, the shirts and suits of his younger days. To Jamie, these clothes represented a lost legacy, what his own life was missing, the lush smell of a father. Jamie ran his fingers over these clothes and tried them on for the mirror, shirts and ties, boots and loafers. As my father was heavier than Jamie, the shoulders of the shirts sagged. Jamie rolled the sleeves and cuffed the pants. He wore the clothes to town, a ragged ghost, a reflection. So good as a kid, he did not have the patience or stamina to be an adult. His mad energy had dwindled. He was twenty-seven.

Jamie bought a 1974 Plymouth Road Runner, which he drove to the beach. It had a blue velvet interior. He had become an infamous figure in town. Cruising the streets, brimming with desperation, he would share sultry looks with the sweet young mothers of suburbia and bring them back to the house and take them to my parents' bed. Afterward, he lay in the dark, hoping his life would take shape. He prayed for a catastrophe—an earthquake, a war, anything that might shake the world free and put his life back in play. I would get calls from friends: "Have you heard about Jamie? It's all my mother talks about. He's being passed around by the women of the village." When I asked Jamie, he sighed and said, "Well, little brother, there is just no one else here to play with."

In 1996, my father at last closed a deal on the house, which had been on the market for over four years. On occasion, my father had used Jamie as a negotiating ploy, dismissing an unacceptable offer by saying, "Sell? For that price? Why should I sell? Why should I make a homeless man of Jamie?" Of course, that is just what the sale did do to Jamie—the loss of a home, the end of an idyll. The prospect of moving back in with his mother and grandmother was ominous. It seemed like a failure. For some time, Jamie had been aware of his symbolic place in my life and in the life of kids up and down the shore. His every hesitation, his every misstep registered, to us, as a generational failure—another lesson delivered. In the house on the Bluffs, he had been able to escape such expectations and vanish into a parallel existence. On the phone, he told me, "I have been living the life of old Glencoe, as one of the chosen, and now I must go back into the world. But I have nothing to give the world. And so what will the world make of me?"

I told him I would be home to box up my possessions. We would have a few days in the house before my parents flew in to ship the furniture. He picked me up at the airport, and we went bouncing off down the highway. Jamie was wearing a silk shirt covered with birds. He was the same as ever, smiling, slapping at the wheel, looking at the green fields fattening with summer. And still, there had been a change—some hardening of his features. When you are a kid and you make a face, your mother says, "Your face will freeze like that." Of course, this is only to scare you, but that really is what happens—your face *does* freeze like that! Depending on luck and experience, in your twenties or thirties or forties, your face settles into a distillation of all the faces you ever made.

We drove into Glencoe. There were trendy stores and tremendous new houses that filled the modest lots property line to property line. The town looked as if it had been torn down and redrawn from memory, refashioned for a new race of men, which, I suppose, it had. "And now," said Jamie. "I will take you to the saddest place I know."

In the center of town, on the former site of Sloppy Ed's, there was a food court, a collection of restaurants with phony, regionless, market-tested names: Godfather's Pizza, because mobsters are Italian and Italians love pizza; Wall Street Deli, because Wall Street is in New York and New Yorkers love deli; Wok & Roll—Oh, those punny Chinese!—Einstein's Bagels, because bagels are Jewish, and who is the smartest Jew the world has ever known? As we ordered, women at the tables, surrounded by families, watched Jamie, some smiling, some frowning. Jamie told me he came here several times a week—because he hated it, because he wanted to remember what he lost, because he was teaching himself there is beauty even here. "It's like a brand-new kitchen table made to look a hundred years old," he explained. "Or like people in the city writing in cafés, or like the McRib sandwich at McDonald's. It's fake as hell but it's all we got, and it tastes pretty good, so eat up!"

For the next several days, Jamie and I went through the house, running up and down stairs, digging through drawers, packing up, throwing out. On a closet in my parents' room Jamie taped a note that read *Everything inside here belongs to Jamie.* One afternoon, when he was in town getting us lunch, I opened the door. Jamie's clothes were lined in neat rows, linen pants and silk shirts I remembered from high school, but also clothes that belonged to my father—suits, shoes, jackets. Seeing those things, I felt a rush of anger in every way disproportionate to the crime. It was as if, by claiming my father's clothes, Jamie was taking something from me. By the time he got back with the food, I had weeded out my father's clothes and thrown them across the bed.

When Jamie saw the clothes, he flushed. "Why are you going through my things?"

"That's just it," I said. "These are not your things. I want to know why they were in your closet."

"Those things were left behind," said Jamie. "I was here and no one was wearing them, and so I took care of them and now they are my things."

I was as angry at Jamie as I have ever been at anyone. I had my fists at my sides.

"You know what?" he said. "You're a greedy sonofabitch."

He turned and left the house. He did not come back and I did not care that he did not come back. A few days later my parents came home and settled into their bedroom. I slept in the attic. It was as if the clock had been pushed back and everything was as it had been. My father asked why he had not seen Jamie. When I told him, he said, "Oh, Richard, what's wrong with you? Jamie can have those clothes. Jamie can have whatever he wants."

I went to Jamie's house the next afternoon. His mother said he was at work and asked me inside for lunch. The windows were open, and a breeze blew from the lake. Jamie's mother moved from sink to refrigerator. In the way that parents never seem to age but, instead, track against the distance like a landmark, she looked the same as ever: sandy blond hair, sharp green eyes. She said she was worried about Jamie. "What will he do?"

I asked about Jamie's life in Glencoe, at work, at school. Then I said, "Do you know what happened to Jamie after high school?"

"What do you mean?"

"Well, after graduation he went off to swim in the Pacific Ocean," I said. "But I never heard from him, and when he got back he was in such a gloomy mood and he never did tell me if he made it out to California."

She looked out the window and made clucking noises that told me she was trying to remember. "Well, yes, Jamie did take a trip, but it was not to California," she said. "He went to Wyoming. In fact, he went out there to see his father."

"His father?"

For a moment I was dazed.

Then I said, "It had been my understanding that Jamie's father died when Jamie was very young."

"Oh, no," said Mrs. Drew. "He builds houses in Casper."

"Why does Jamie talk as if his father were dead?"

Mrs. Drew considered the question. "Well, his father is not a very pleasant man," she said. "Jamie went out there unannounced, and his father—he has his new life and his new family, after all, so how can he be bothered with Jamie?—put him on the first bus back early the next morning. He just couldn't wait to get rid of him."

Over the next few days, working at the house, I thought about this new information. It was like a splash of color that changes the entire picture. It explained the longing that made up so much of Jamie's personality. His relationship with his father, a relationship that was expressed, like man's relationship with God, mostly by its absence, was, after all, the great sunless center of his being. His father even spoke in the voice of God—that is, in silence. I imagined Jamie heading toward that distant encounter, down empty highways, with hopes vague and thrilling. Those hopes were with him in lonely hotel rooms, crickets in the grass, a vacancy sign in the window; he carried them into the foothills. And at last he saw his father for the first time in years, a slim-hipped hero of the snowy west—a man of that American generation that somehow let it all slip away. Jamie slept on the couch and in the morning was on his way home, flat-land wilderness wandering past the windows of the bus.

The day before I was to return to New York, Jamie
showed up at the house. He did not say anything about
our fight or about my discussion with his mother. Did he
know that I knew? I did not ask. I have always found it difficult to bring up any subject that might make anyone,
especially a friend, uncomfortable. And Jamie was more
than my friend. He was what, for years, looking in a mirror, I had hoped to see looking back at me.

When Jamie realized I would not question him, he said,
"I have something to show you."

In the attic, he removed a panel that covered our
favorite high school hiding place. Against the wall, glazed
with dust, was a six of Mickey's big mouth. "It must have
been up here for ten years," said Jamie.

We opened a bottle out in the yard. It fizzed like crazy.
We each took a sip. It was warm and skunky.

Jamie said, "Let's go to the city."

I made some calls, and a few friends from New York
who happened to be visiting Chicago agreed to meet us,
and so did Ronnie, who was living downtown. We met
at a bar in Lincoln Park. Ronnie was wearing a dark Italian suit and talking interest rates. He had taken a job
at some kind of mutual fund. Each time I saw him, he
looked more sure of himself, more prosperous. That night
I realized Ronnie would surely be the most successful of
my friends. He was protected by a strange confidence—
the confidence of someone who, as a boy, had spoken
to God.

At some point, we started drinking. We drank in the bars, in the streets, in the back of an underground club. The liquor got us talking and joking and racing from discussion to discussion. In the club, which was in a basement on the West Side, there were girls in bell-bottoms and belly shirts. Jamie said he was appalled by the retrocraze. "It's regressive," he explained. "It means you are out of ideas, have surrendered to the past, have convinced yourself time has stopped." Wearing such clothes, he explained, requires an industrial-strength irony, a joke so finely tuned it forgets it's a joke. "So you see, these people are not actually living in the world but in a muddy reflection of the world." That led him to the subject of multitasking, wherein people, in one moment, perform two tasks: talk to the bank, fold the laundry. "The age of the multitask is a bankrupt age," said Jamie. "It's an age in which, by trying to have two experiences simultaneously, you ruin both and so have no experience at all."

At some point, as we leaned over a bar, I remember thinking, Why can't we go on like this forever? Why can't we be free? If we had no parents, I decided, we could be free. If we had no one to answer to, if we were truly adults, if we were autonomous, if we could make our way free of role models and lessons and expectations, free of grandparents and photo albums, free of heredity—but we can never be that free.

The night ended at Ronnie's apartment, what you

would call a closer, the sun rising at the end of the street. As Jamie and I talked, Ronnie stretched and yawned. One of my friends from New York said, "I think Ronnie wants us to leave."

"We've wanted Ronnie to leave for twenty-five years," I said. "We're staying."

Much later, riding the train with Jamie, I said, "When my parents go to Washington, you should get out of Glencoe too. Just take off."

When I got back to New York, there was a message on my machine. It was from Jamie. I could hear the highway at his back. He shouted, "Hey, little brother! I'm standing on a corner in Winslow, Arizona. I'm heading out to Los Angeles. I'm gonna reach that beach."

Over the last few years, most of my old friends have gotten married and settled down. Some have even moved back to Glencoe. It rises from the suburbs, and so it returns. At first these friends went in bunches, two or three a season. I would speak of them the way people once spoke of wild Indians who at last settled on the reservation as having "come in." Or as Missouri lawmen spoke of Frank James, upon his surrender, as having come in. "It is for the best that old Frank James has come in." Or as we spoke of those kids who, after dinner on a summer night, had been told to come in, leaving just a few of us on the street.

Sometimes, if I cannot sleep, I look at pictures of those friends. Tom Pistone, married with two kids, his once-beloved Pontiac GTO rotting in the grass behind his house. Ronnie at his wedding, wearing a bow tie because he always had a Frank Sinatra image of himself at his wedding with his bow tie undone. Rink Anderson in a church out west, a mountain rising steeply in the door.

Or I look at pictures of the Glencoe beach or downtown Chicago, or at a picture that Jamie snapped at a Cubs game—infielders moving with the pitch, the batter stepping into the swing, the catcher on his toes, the ball hanging ten feet off the plate.

If I still cannot sleep, I think of all the years I have already put behind me. To give a face to these years, I think of all the girls I ever slept with, all the girls I ever kissed, starting with Paige Morrison in a field behind North School, her skirt riding up—or was it that girl from Deerfield, who put me down like a prison riot?—and then of every person I have ever known. Or I think of my signature, which my father helped me invent on a couch in Skokie, Illinois, in the house of my grandmother's second husband, Izzy Blustein, a stooped little man who had lied about his age and died less than a year after the wedding, causing my brother to say, "Izzy come, Izzy go." That signature is looped and curled, and my father said, "Now you can be famous." I think of all the times I have scribbled that signature and of all the places I have left it—at gas stations and bars and hotel lobbies—a ghostly image of my passing.

About a year ago, I saw Jamie in New York. For a thousand dollars, he had driven a truck from Los Angeles, dropped it off in midtown, come to my apartment, told me about some of the things he had seen on the road, including London Bridge in Lake Havasu City, Arizona, and then stretched out on my bed and gone to sleep. By this time, I myself was married. When I got married, I felt that my relationship with my old friends had somehow changed. Even when we went out, the night was no longer open to us in quite the same way. Getting married had not caused this change, but it did seem to acknowledge it. It was like signing a treaty for a war that ended long ago. When Jessica came home from work, I brought her in to see my famous friend Jamie. He was face up on the bed, skin dark and smooth. In high school, I explained, Jamie's most memorable antics were talked about and told and analyzed and commented on and retold, until they became legends. I said, "This is what my friend looks like sleeping."

When Jamie woke up, we went out for a drink at a neighborhood bar. Jamie ordered Jack Daniel's and talked about his life in Los Angeles. He said he was working as a carpenter, designing and building the sets of B-movies. He said this life might sound boring to us, but that he was in fact living it fully and with great passion. "I have tremendous respect for ordinary lives, like the one I'm now living," he explained. "Such a life is like a song that, in high school, you were too cool for, like 'The Devil Went Down to Georgia,' but that, if you really listen to it, you have to admit it really is a pretty good song. It is sweet and funny and you can dance to it, and really, what more do you want from a song?"

We headed to the Port Authority, where Jamie had to catch a bus back to L.A. A job was waiting. It was one of those strange summer nights in the city when the sky rides high and everyone on the street looks famous. This is just the kind of thing Jamie would have once noticed, but he did not seem to care. This is the problem with writing about people—people change, as cities change, as families change, as even the past changes, forever weaving itself into a new pattern. At best you can hope to capture a single moment, like a lightning bug in an overturned glass.

Jamie tossed his bag over his shoulder and climbed onto the bus and waved in the window as it drove away.

Acknowledgments

Writing this book was really fun and I want to thank all the people who helped me with it. My sister Sharon and my brother Steven, who is in the process of raising that long hoped for messiah, the Jewish Bobby Orr. I want to thank Bill Levin, Lisa Melmed and Robert Blumenthal, and also my friends Jim Albrecht, Ian Frazier, Alec Wilkinson, David Lipsky and C. S. Ledbetter III, a colossus of American letters; my agent, Andrew Wylie, and Jeff Posternak, also at the Wylie agency; all the people at Knopf but especially Jordan Pavlin, my editor, who really should visit the great city of Chicago. And, while I'm at it, I might as well thank Chicago too! Thanks for everything, Chicago, but especially for the redhots and the Cubs! I also want to thank my mother, who, whenever I demanded a birthday present, used to say, "Your whole life is a gift." I was stupid then, but now I know that she was right. My father, for his yellow legal pads and his red pens, for his never-ending belief that there is still time for law school. I also want to thank every kid I grew up with, even the ones I was mean to and even the ones who were mean to me. Thanks for not turning me in to the principal, for coming over on a weeknight, for letting me see your test, for letting me date your sister, for lending me your car, for buying me beer. Some of these friends I still talk to but most are scattered. Where are you, Vooch? And what about you, Todd? You were my best friend. And Jenny and Becky, I've got some really funny stuff to tell you. Spitzer is still around, but what ever happened to Rocket? Of course, I also want to thank my wife, Jessica, who stood on the other side of this story like the prize in the Cracker Jack box. It has been more fun than a day at Coney Island.

A NOTE ABOUT THE AUTHOR

Rich Cohen has written for *The New Yorker* and the *New York Times Magazine,* among many other publications. He is a contributing editor at *Rolling Stone* and recently cowrote a film script with Martin Scorsese and Mick Jagger. He lives in New York City.

A NOTE ON THE TYPE

This book was set in Janson, a typeface long thought to have been made by the Dutchman Anton Janson, who was a practicing type-founder in Leipzig during the years 1668–1687. However, it has been conclusively demonstrated that these types are actually the work of Nicholas Kis (1650–1702), a Hungarian, who most probably learned his trade from the master Dutch typefounder Dirk Voskens. The type is an excellent example of the influential and sturdy Dutch types that prevailed in England up to the time William Caslon (1692–1766) developed his own incomparable designs from them.

Composed by Creative Graphics, Inc., Allentown, Pennsylvania
Printed and bound by R. R. Donnelley & Sons, Harrisonburg, Virginia
Designed by Robert C. Olsson